Positive Habits: Small Steps to Big Change

Shah Rukh

Published by Shah Rukh, 2024.

While every precaution has been taken in the preparation of this book, the publisher assumes no responsibility for errors or omissions, or for damages resulting from the use of the information contained herein.

POSITIVE HABITS: SMALL STEPS TO BIG CHANGE

First edition. May 20, 2024.

Copyright © 2024 Shah Rukh.

Written by Shah Rukh.

Table of Contents

Prologue...1

Chapter 1: Introduction...3

Chapter 2: Understanding Habits 7

Chapter 3: Setting the Foundation.....................11

Chapter 4: Morning Rituals 16

Chapter 5: Evening Routines 19

Chapter 6: The Art of Goal Setting....................22

Chapter 7: Mindful Living..................................25

Chapter 8: Exercise and Movement....................28

Chapter 9: Healthy Eating..................................31

Chapter 10: Sleep Hygiene..................................34

Chapter 11: Stress Management 37

Chapter 12: Productivity Hacks 40

Chapter 13: Time Management 42

Chapter 14: Building Resilience..........................44

Chapter 15: Gratitude Practice 47

Chapter 16: Positive Thinking.............................49

Chapter 17: Self-Care Strategies 52

Chapter 18: Building Strong Relationships.........54

Chapter 19: The Power of Saying No...................57

Chapter 20: Financial Wellness...........................60

Chapter 21: Lifelong Learning............................63

Chapter 22: Creative Expression.........................66

Chapter 23: Decluttering Your Space 69

Chapter 24: Digital Detox...................................72

Chapter 25: Mindful Consumption....................75

Chapter 26: Altruism and Volunteering.............78

Chapter 27: Developing Patience 81

Chapter 28: Overcoming Procrastination...........84

Chapter 29: Building a Support Network............87

Chapter 30: Habit Stacking 90

Chapter 31: Embracing Change 93

Chapter 32: Mindful Breathing 96

Chapter 33: Visualization Techniques 99

Chapter 34: Journaling for Growth 101

Chapter 35: The Role of Humor 103

Chapter 36: Spiritual Practices 105

Chapter 37: Finding Balance 108

Chapter 38: Celebrating Small Wins 111

Chapter 39: Sustaining Motivation 113

Chapter 40: Conclusion 115

Epilogue 117

Prologue

In the vast landscape of our lives, where dreams take root and aspirations flourish, lies the potential for profound transformation. It is within the intricate tapestry of our daily habits that the seeds of change are sown, where small actions, repeated consistently, yield remarkable results. Welcome to "Positive Habits: Small Steps to Big Change," a journey into the heart of personal growth and transformation.

In the hustle and bustle of modern life, it's easy to lose sight of the power of our habits—the daily rituals and routines that shape our thoughts, actions, and ultimately, our destinies. Yet, hidden within the seemingly mundane fabric of our everyday lives lies the key to unlocking our greatest potential and living our fullest, most vibrant lives.

In this book, we embark on a journey of discovery, exploration, and empowerment, as we uncover the transformative power of positive habits. Drawing on the latest research in psychology, neuroscience, and behavioral science, we delve into the science behind habit formation, exploring how small changes in behavior can lead to significant improvements in every area of our lives.

But this book is more than just a compilation of scientific facts and figures—it's a practical guidebook for personal growth and development, offering actionable insights, strategies, and exercises to help you cultivate positive habits and create lasting change. Whether you're looking to improve your health, boost your productivity, or enhance your relationships, you'll find practical tips and techniques to help you harness the power of small steps to achieve big results.

Through inspiring stories, real-life examples, and thought-provoking exercises, we'll explore the art and science of habit formation, uncovering the secrets to creating lasting change in our lives. From the importance of setting clear goals and intentions to the role of mindfulness and self-awareness in habit formation, we'll explore the key principles and practices that will empower you to take control of your habits and transform your life.

So, if you're ready to embark on a journey of personal growth and transformation, if you're ready to unleash your fullest potential and create the life you've always dreamed of, then join us on this journey of discovery, as we explore the power of positive habits and the small steps that lead to big change. The journey begins now—let's take the first step together.

Chapter 1: Introduction

The journey of self-improvement often seems daunting, primarily because of the sheer scale of change required. However, understanding the power of small steps can transform this journey into a manageable and rewarding process. The essence of small steps lies in their simplicity and attainability, breaking down significant goals into smaller, actionable tasks. This approach not only makes the path to success less overwhelming but also builds a sense of accomplishment and momentum over time.

Human nature often gravitates towards immediate results. This inclination can make us set grand, ambitious goals with the hope of rapid transformation. However, the reality is that such drastic changes are rarely sustainable. When we aim for enormous leaps, the effort required can lead to burnout, frustration, and eventual abandonment of the goal. Conversely, small steps allow for gradual progress, making the process feel more manageable and less intimidating. Each small step serves as a building block, creating a solid foundation for long-term success.

One of the key principles of the power of small steps is the concept of incremental improvement. This principle is vividly illustrated in the Japanese philosophy of Kaizen, which translates to "continuous improvement." Kaizen emphasizes that small, consistent changes can lead to significant improvement over time. By focusing on making minor adjustments and improvements daily, the cumulative effect can be profound. This approach is not only applicable to personal development but is also widely used in business and manufacturing to enhance efficiency and quality.

Psychologically, small steps play a crucial role in maintaining motivation. Large goals can seem unattainable and may lead to procrastination or a sense of defeat even before starting. In contrast, breaking these goals into smaller, more manageable tasks makes the process seem less daunting. Each small step completed provides a sense of achievement, reinforcing the belief that progress is possible. This reinforcement builds confidence and creates a positive feedback loop, where success breeds further success.

Furthermore, small steps allow for the development of new habits. According to research in behavioral psychology, habits are formed through repetition and consistency. By taking small, regular actions, these behaviors become ingrained over time, turning into habits. For example, if someone aims to become more physically fit, starting with a small, manageable exercise routine, like a 10-minute daily walk, can be more effective in establishing a lasting habit than attempting an intensive workout regimen from the outset.

Another significant advantage of small steps is their ability to adapt to life's unpredictability. Life is rarely linear, and unforeseen challenges often arise. Large, rigid plans can crumble in the face of such obstacles, leading to discouragement and a sense of failure. Small steps, however, offer flexibility. When circumstances change, it's easier to adjust small tasks than to overhaul a grand plan. This adaptability ensures continuous progress, even in the face of setbacks.

The power of small steps is also evident in skill acquisition. Learning a new skill can be overwhelming, especially when considering the gap between the current state and the desired level of proficiency. By breaking down the learning process into smaller, more manageable components, the task becomes less overwhelming. For instance, learning a new language can start with mastering a few basic phrases daily rather than attempting to become fluent in a short period. Each small achievement builds confidence and lays the groundwork for further learning.

Moreover, the concept of small steps is supported by numerous success stories and real-life examples. Entrepreneurs, athletes, and successful individuals across various fields often attribute their accomplishments to consistent, incremental progress rather than sudden, massive efforts. This approach ensures that progress is sustainable and growth is continuous. It also highlights the importance of perseverance and patience, demonstrating that lasting success is built over time.

In addition to individual benefits, the power of small steps can influence group dynamics and collective efforts. In team settings, breaking down large projects into smaller tasks can improve collaboration and efficiency. Each team member can focus on specific, manageable tasks, leading to a more coordinated and productive effort. This approach also fosters a sense of shared achievement, enhancing morale and motivation within the group.

To harness the power of small steps effectively, it's essential to set clear, specific goals. Vague goals can lead to confusion and lack of direction, while precise, well-defined goals provide a roadmap for progress. It's also important to celebrate small victories along the way. Recognizing and rewarding incremental achievements reinforces positive behavior and keeps motivation high.

Additionally, maintaining a long-term perspective is crucial. While small steps focus on immediate, manageable actions, keeping the bigger picture in mind ensures that these actions are aligned with the ultimate goal. Regularly reviewing and adjusting the plan helps maintain this alignment and ensures continuous progress toward the desired outcome.

The power of small steps is a transformative approach to self-improvement and goal achievement. By breaking down large, intimidating goals into smaller, manageable tasks, the journey becomes less overwhelming and more sustainable. This approach fosters incremental improvement, builds confidence and motivation, develops new habits, and offers flexibility in the face of challenges. It is a strategy supported by psychological principles, real-life success stories, and practical application in both individual and group settings. Embracing the power of small steps can lead to profound and lasting change, demonstrating that even the most ambitious goals are attainable with consistent, incremental progress.

Chapter 2: Understanding Habits

Understanding habits involves delving into the science of behavior, a field that encompasses psychology, neuroscience, and even sociology. Habits are the routines and behaviors we perform almost automatically, and they shape a significant part of our daily lives. They can be both beneficial and detrimental, influencing everything from our productivity and health to our social interactions and mental well-being. To truly grasp the science of habits, we need to explore how they are formed, maintained, and changed, drawing on a variety of scientific perspectives.

At the core of habit formation is a neurological process called the habit loop, which consists of three main components: cue, routine, and reward. This concept was popularized by Charles Duhigg in his book "The Power of Habit." The cue is the trigger that initiates the behavior; it can be anything from a specific time of day, an emotional state, a location, or the presence of certain people. The routine is the behavior itself, the action that follows the cue. Finally, the reward is the positive outcome or benefit we get from the behavior, which reinforces the habit and makes it more likely to be repeated in the future.

Neuroscientific research has identified that the basal ganglia, a group of nuclei in the brain, play a crucial role in habit formation. When a new habit is being formed, the brain is highly active, especially in the decision-making areas such as the prefrontal cortex. However, as the behavior becomes more ingrained, the brain activity shifts towards the basal ganglia, making the behavior more automatic and less cognitively demanding. This shift allows the brain to conserve energy and resources, which is why habits can be so powerful and difficult to break.

One of the most fascinating aspects of habits is their persistence. Once a habit is formed, it can remain dormant for years, only to be reactivated by the right cue. This persistence is due to the way our brains consolidate habitual behaviors into our neural architecture. Even if a habit has not been practiced for a long time, the neural pathways associated with it can remain intact, ready to be reactivated. This is why old habits often resurface, especially under stress or in familiar environments.

The concept of keystone habits further elucidates the power of habits in shaping our behavior. Keystone habits are those that, once adopted, tend to lead to the development of other positive habits. For example, regular exercise is considered a keystone habit because it can trigger improvements in other areas such as eating habits, productivity, and even sleep patterns. The success of keystone habits lies in their ability to create a ripple effect, initiating a chain reaction of positive changes.

Understanding the science of habits also involves recognizing the role of reinforcement and repetition. The theory of operant conditioning, developed by B.F. Skinner, highlights how behaviors that are reinforced tend to be repeated. Positive reinforcement, where a behavior is followed by a rewarding stimulus, strengthens the habit loop. Negative reinforcement, which involves the removal of an aversive stimulus following a behavior, can also reinforce habits. Both types of reinforcement play a crucial role in maintaining and strengthening habits over time.

Repetition is another critical factor in habit formation. The more frequently a behavior is repeated in the same context, the more likely it is to become automatic. Studies suggest that it can take anywhere from 18 to 254 days to form a new habit, with an average of around 66 days. This variation depends on the complexity of the behavior, individual differences, and consistency in performing the behavior. The process of habit formation is non-linear, meaning that initial progress might be slow, but with consistent repetition, the behavior eventually becomes automatic.

Changing habits, especially breaking bad ones, involves disrupting the habit loop and replacing the routine with a more desirable behavior. This process often requires conscious effort and persistence. One effective strategy is to identify and modify the cues and rewards associated with the habit. For instance, if the habit is snacking on unhealthy foods when feeling stressed, one might replace the routine of snacking with a healthier alternative like drinking water or taking a walk, while still addressing the same cue (stress) and achieving a positive reward (relief from stress).

Another important aspect of habit change is leveraging social support and accountability. Sharing goals with friends, family, or support groups can provide motivation and encouragement. Social support networks can help reinforce positive behaviors and offer assistance in overcoming obstacles. Additionally, monitoring progress and celebrating small victories can boost motivation and reinforce the new habit.

Cognitive-behavioral strategies are also effective in habit change. Techniques such as self-monitoring, where individuals track their behavior and identify patterns, can increase awareness and facilitate change. Cognitive restructuring, which involves challenging and altering negative thought patterns that trigger undesirable habits, can also be beneficial. By changing the underlying thoughts and beliefs associated with a habit, individuals can alter their behavior more effectively.

The concept of willpower and self-control is closely linked to habit formation and change. Willpower is often described as a finite resource that can be depleted; a phenomenon known as ego depletion. However, some research suggests that viewing willpower as a non-limited resource can enhance self-control. Strengthening willpower through practices such as mindfulness, stress management, and adequate rest can support habit change efforts. Building habits gradually, starting with small, manageable changes, can also help conserve willpower and increase the likelihood of success.

The environment plays a significant role in shaping habits. Environmental cues can strongly influence behavior, often more so than conscious intentions. Modifying the environment to reduce exposure to cues that trigger unwanted habits and increase exposure to cues that promote desired habits can facilitate habit change. For instance, keeping healthy snacks visible and easily accessible while removing unhealthy options from the immediate environment can support dietary changes.

Incorporating habit-tracking tools and technology can aid in habit formation and change. Apps and digital tools that provide reminders, track progress, and offer rewards can enhance motivation and consistency. These tools can help individuals stay accountable and provide data that can be used to refine and adjust strategies as needed.

Understanding the science of habits involves a multidisciplinary approach that encompasses psychological, neurological, and environmental factors. Habits are formed through a process known as the habit loop, which involves cues, routines, and rewards, and are reinforced by repetition and positive outcomes. The persistence of habits is due to their consolidation in the brain's neural architecture, making them powerful and often resistant to change. Keystone habits, reinforcement, and repetition are crucial in habit formation, while modifying cues and rewards, leveraging social support, and employing cognitive-behavioral strategies are effective in changing habits. Willpower, environmental influences, and technological tools also play significant roles in shaping and modifying our habits. By understanding and applying these principles, individuals can harness the power of habits to achieve personal growth and improve their overall quality of life.

Chapter 3: Setting the Foundation

Creating a positive mindset is a fundamental component of personal development and overall well-being. A positive mindset not only enhances mental and emotional health but also contributes to physical health, resilience, and success in various aspects of life. Setting the foundation for a positive mindset involves understanding the underlying principles of positivity, recognizing the benefits, and implementing practical strategies to cultivate and maintain a positive outlook.

At its core, a positive mindset is characterized by an optimistic attitude, constructive thinking patterns, and an overall sense of well-being. It involves focusing on the good in any given situation, maintaining hope and confidence about the future, and viewing challenges as opportunities for growth. Developing a positive mindset requires a conscious effort to shift from negative to positive thinking, fostering habits that reinforce optimism and resilience.

One of the key principles of a positive mindset is the concept of neuroplasticity, which is the brain's ability to reorganize itself by forming new neural connections throughout life. This ability means that even ingrained patterns of negative thinking can be changed. By consistently practicing positive thinking and behaviors, individuals can create new, healthier neural pathways. This process not only changes how one thinks but also how one feels and behaves, leading to a more positive and fulfilling life.

The benefits of a positive mindset are well-documented in scientific research. Studies have shown that individuals with a positive outlook are more likely to experience better physical health, including lower rates of cardiovascular disease, stronger immune systems, and longer lifespans. Mental health benefits include lower levels of stress, anxiety, and depression. Positive thinking also enhances cognitive functions such as creativity, problem-solving, and decision-making, contributing to success in personal and professional endeavors.

Cultivating a positive mindset begins with self-awareness and mindfulness. Self-awareness involves recognizing and understanding one's thoughts, emotions, and behaviors. Mindfulness, the practice of being present and fully engaged in the current moment, helps in becoming aware of negative thought patterns as they arise. By acknowledging these patterns without judgment, individuals can start to challenge and change them.

One practical strategy to foster a positive mindset is the practice of gratitude. Gratitude involves recognizing and appreciating the good things in life, no matter how small. Keeping a gratitude journal, where one writes down things they are thankful for each day, can significantly enhance one's overall sense of positivity and well-being. Research indicates that gratitude practices can increase happiness, reduce stress, and improve relationships.

Positive affirmations are another effective tool. These are positive statements that individuals repeat to themselves to challenge and overcome negative thoughts. Affirmations can be tailored to address specific areas of negativity and reinforce positive self-beliefs. For example, someone struggling with self-doubt might use affirmations such as, "I am capable and confident," or "I trust in my abilities." Over time, these affirmations can help rewire the brain to adopt more positive thinking patterns.

Visualization, the practice of imagining oneself achieving goals and experiencing positive outcomes, can also help in creating a positive mindset. Visualization harnesses the power of the mind to create mental images of success, which can enhance motivation and confidence. By regularly visualizing positive scenarios, individuals can build a stronger belief in their ability to achieve their goals, thereby increasing the likelihood of success.

Engaging in regular physical activity is another cornerstone of developing a positive mindset. Exercise has been shown to release endorphins, the body's natural mood elevators. Regular physical activity can reduce stress, anxiety, and depression, while also boosting self-esteem and cognitive function. Finding an enjoyable form of exercise, whether it be walking, yoga, dancing, or sports, can make it easier to incorporate into daily routines.

Social connections play a significant role in fostering a positive mindset. Building and maintaining strong relationships with family, friends, and the community provides emotional support, increases feelings of belonging, and enhances overall happiness. Positive social interactions can serve as a buffer against stress and adversity, making it easier to maintain a positive outlook even in challenging times. Acts of kindness, whether giving or receiving, can also boost positive emotions and strengthen social bonds.

Developing resilience is a crucial aspect of maintaining a positive mindset. Resilience is the ability to bounce back from adversity and setbacks. It involves adopting a growth mindset, which is the belief that abilities and intelligence can be developed through effort and learning. Resilient individuals view challenges as opportunities to grow and learn rather than as insurmountable obstacles. Building resilience involves practicing self-compassion, setting realistic goals, and maintaining a sense of purpose.

Mindfulness meditation is another powerful practice for cultivating a positive mindset. Meditation involves focusing the mind and eliminating distractions to achieve a state of calm and clarity. Mindfulness meditation, in particular, emphasizes being present and fully accepting the current moment without judgment. Regular practice can help reduce negative thinking, increase self-awareness, and enhance emotional regulation. This can lead to greater overall positivity and improved mental health.

It's also important to manage and reduce exposure to negativity. This can include setting boundaries with negative individuals, limiting consumption of negative news or social media, and creating a positive physical environment. Surrounding oneself with positivity, such as inspirational books, uplifting music, and affirming decorations, can reinforce a positive mindset.

Developing a positive mindset also involves setting and working towards meaningful goals. Goal-setting provides direction and purpose, which are essential for maintaining motivation and positivity. Breaking down larger goals into smaller, manageable tasks can make the process less overwhelming and more achievable. Celebrating small achievements along the way can boost confidence and reinforce positive behavior.

Self-care is another vital component of creating a positive mindset. Taking time to care for one's physical, emotional, and mental well-being is essential for maintaining a positive outlook. This can include activities such as adequate rest, balanced nutrition, relaxation techniques, and hobbies that bring joy and fulfillment.

Learning and personal growth contribute significantly to a positive mindset. Engaging in continuous learning, whether through formal education, reading, or new experiences, can foster a sense of accomplishment and purpose. Personal growth involves stepping out of one's comfort zone and embracing new challenges, which can build confidence and resilience.

Finally, it's important to practice self-compassion. Self-compassion involves treating oneself with kindness and understanding during times of failure or difficulty. Instead of harsh self-criticism, self-compassion encourages a more forgiving and nurturing attitude. This can help reduce negative self-talk and enhance overall positivity.

Creating a positive mindset is a multifaceted process that involves self-awareness, gratitude, positive affirmations, visualization, physical activity, social connections, resilience, mindfulness meditation, managing negativity, goal-setting, self-care, continuous learning, and self-compassion. By incorporating these strategies into daily life, individuals can set a strong foundation for a positive mindset, leading to improved mental, emotional, and physical well-being. Embracing positivity not only enhances personal happiness but also fosters a more fulfilling and successful life.

Chapter 4: Morning Rituals

Morning rituals are powerful routines that set the tone for the rest of the day, influencing productivity, mood, and overall well-being. By intentionally crafting a morning ritual, individuals can create a positive and energizing start to their day, enhancing focus, motivation, and resilience. These rituals encompass a variety of activities aimed at nourishing the body, mind, and spirit, and they can vary widely depending on personal preferences and lifestyle. Setting the stage for a successful day begins with understanding the importance of morning rituals and incorporating practices that resonate with individual needs and goals.

The significance of morning rituals lies in their ability to provide structure and stability in an otherwise chaotic world. In today's fast-paced society, mornings often set the tone for the rest of the day. A rushed or chaotic morning can lead to feelings of stress, overwhelm, and disorganization, making it difficult to focus and perform at optimal levels. Conversely, a mindful and intentional morning ritual can create a sense of calm, clarity, and purpose, laying the foundation for a productive and fulfilling day ahead.

Morning rituals can vary widely from person to person, but they often include a combination of activities aimed at nurturing the body, mind, and spirit. Physical practices such as exercise, stretching, or yoga can help wake up the body, increase energy levels, and improve overall health and well-being. Engaging in movement first thing in the morning can also boost mood and mental clarity, setting a positive tone for the day ahead.

Nutrition is another important aspect of morning rituals. Starting the day with a nutritious breakfast provides the body with essential nutrients and energy to fuel physical and mental activities. This can include a balanced meal consisting of protein, healthy fats, complex carbohydrates, and fiber. Hydration is also key, as drinking water upon waking helps rehydrate the body after hours of sleep and kickstarts metabolism.

Mindfulness practices such as meditation, deep breathing, or journaling can help cultivate a sense of calm and focus, reducing stress and anxiety. Taking a few moments for quiet reflection or setting positive intentions for the day can promote a positive mindset and emotional resilience. Additionally, reading or listening to inspirational content can stimulate the mind and provide motivation and inspiration for the day ahead.

Establishing a morning ritual involves consistency and intentionality. By committing to a set of practices each morning, individuals create a sense of routine and predictability that can enhance productivity and reduce decision fatigue. Consistency is key to forming habits, and over time, morning rituals become automatic and ingrained in daily life.

The benefits of morning rituals extend beyond the immediate effects on mood and productivity. Research suggests that starting the day with positive habits can have a ripple effect, influencing behavior and decision-making throughout the day. For example, individuals who exercise in the morning are more likely to make healthier food choices and engage in other positive behaviors throughout the day. Similarly, practicing gratitude or setting intentions in the morning can cultivate a mindset of positivity and resilience that carries through challenges and setbacks.

Morning rituals also provide an opportunity for self-care and personal growth. By dedicating time to activities that nourish the body, mind, and spirit, individuals prioritize their own well-being and set themselves up for success in all areas of life. This can include activities such as reading, journaling, practicing gratitude, or engaging in hobbies and interests that bring joy and fulfillment.

Creating a morning ritual is a highly individualized process that requires experimentation and self-awareness. What works for one person may not work for another, so it's important to find practices that resonate with individual preferences, values, and goals. This may involve trying out different activities, routines, and timing to determine what feels most beneficial and sustainable.

It's also important to be flexible and adaptable with morning rituals, recognizing that life can be unpredictable and routines may need to be adjusted from time to time. Instead of viewing disruptions as failures, see them as opportunities to practice resilience and problem-solving. Even on busy or challenging days, finding a few moments for self-care and reflection can make a significant difference in mood and mindset.

Incorporating morning rituals into daily life requires prioritization and commitment. This may involve waking up earlier or rearranging schedules to make time for self-care and personal growth. While it may require some effort and discipline initially, the long-term benefits of morning rituals far outweigh the temporary discomfort of change.

Chapter 5: Evening Routines

Evening routines serve as the bookend to our days, providing closure, relaxation, and preparation for restorative sleep. Crafting an evening routine is essential for ending the day on a high note, promoting relaxation, mindfulness, and a sense of accomplishment. These routines encompass a variety of activities aimed at winding down, reflecting on the day, and preparing for the next day's challenges. Understanding the importance of evening routines and incorporating practices that promote rest and rejuvenation is crucial for overall well-being and success.

The significance of evening routines lies in their ability to facilitate the transition from the busyness of the day to a state of relaxation and rest. In today's fast-paced world, it's common for individuals to feel overwhelmed and stressed by the constant demands of work, family, and other obligations. Evening routines provide an opportunity to slow down, disconnect from technology, and prioritize self-care and relaxation.

One of the key components of an evening routine is establishing a consistent bedtime. Going to bed at the same time each night helps regulate the body's internal clock, promoting better sleep quality and overall health. It's important to create a relaxing bedtime environment free from distractions such as electronic devices, bright lights, and loud noises. This can involve dimming the lights, practicing relaxation techniques such as deep breathing or meditation, and avoiding stimulating activities such as watching TV or scrolling through social media.

Engaging in activities that promote relaxation and stress relief is another essential aspect of evening routines. This can include taking a warm bath or shower, practicing gentle yoga or stretching, or enjoying a calming cup of herbal tea. These activities help signal to the body and mind that it's time to unwind and prepare for sleep.

Reflecting on the day is an important practice that helps individuals process their experiences and emotions. This can involve journaling about the day's events, expressing gratitude for positive moments, or identifying areas for improvement. Reflective practices promote self-awareness and mindfulness, allowing individuals to gain insights into their thoughts, feelings, and behaviors.

Setting intentions for the next day is another beneficial practice that helps individuals feel prepared and organized. This can involve making a to-do list, prioritizing tasks, and setting goals for the following day. By planning ahead, individuals can reduce feelings of stress and overwhelm and approach the day with clarity and purpose.

Creating a relaxing bedtime routine for children is equally important. Establishing consistent bedtime rituals such as reading a bedtime story, taking a warm bath, or practicing relaxation techniques can help children wind down and prepare for sleep. Limiting screen time before bed and creating a calm, soothing environment in the bedroom can also promote better sleep quality.

Incorporating gratitude practices into evening routines can have profound effects on overall well-being. Taking a few moments each night to reflect on the things we are grateful for can shift our focus from what went wrong to what went right, promoting feelings of happiness and contentment. This can involve keeping a gratitude journal, sharing gratitudes with a partner or family members, or simply taking a moment to silently reflect on the day's blessings.

Practicing mindfulness is another valuable component of evening routines. Mindfulness involves paying attention to the present moment with openness, curiosity, and acceptance. This can involve engaging in mindfulness meditation, body scans, or simply tuning in to our senses and noticing the sights, sounds, and sensations around us. Mindfulness practices promote relaxation, reduce stress, and improve overall well-being.

Creating a technology-free zone in the bedroom is essential for promoting restful sleep. The blue light emitted by electronic devices such as smartphones, tablets, and computers can interfere with the body's natural sleep-wake cycle, making it difficult to fall asleep and stay asleep. Establishing a rule of no screens in the bedroom can help create a calm, distraction-free environment conducive to restorative sleep.

Engaging in relaxing activities such as reading a book, listening to soothing music, or practicing gentle yoga can help promote relaxation and prepare the body and mind for sleep. These activities signal to the body that it's time to wind down and prepare for rest.

Establishing a consistent bedtime routine is important for promoting healthy sleep habits. Going to bed at the same time each night and waking up at the same time each morning helps regulate the body's internal clock, promoting better sleep quality and overall well-being. It's also important to create a relaxing bedtime environment free from distractions such as electronic devices, bright lights, and loud noises.

Practicing relaxation techniques such as deep breathing, progressive muscle relaxation, or meditation can help promote relaxation and reduce stress levels. These techniques can be especially helpful for individuals who have difficulty falling asleep due to racing thoughts or anxiety.

Creating a bedtime routine for children is equally important for promoting healthy sleep habits. Establishing consistent bedtime rituals such as reading a bedtime story, taking a warm bath, or practicing relaxation techniques can help children wind down and prepare for sleep. It's also important to create a calm, soothing environment in the bedroom free from distractions such as electronic devices or noisy toys.

Chapter 6: The Art of Goal Setting

The art of goal setting is a transformative process that empowers individuals to clarify their aspirations, create actionable plans, and achieve meaningful success. Setting goals is not merely about envisioning a desired outcome; it's about strategically mapping out the steps necessary to turn dreams into reality. This process involves careful consideration of one's values, priorities, and strengths, as well as an understanding of how to overcome obstacles and stay motivated along the journey. By mastering the art of goal setting, individuals can unlock their full potential and live a life of purpose, fulfillment, and accomplishment.

At the heart of effective goal setting is clarity. Before setting goals, it's essential to take the time to reflect on one's values, passions, and long-term aspirations. What truly matters to you? What do you hope to achieve in the various areas of your life, such as career, relationships, health, and personal growth? By gaining clarity on these questions, individuals can set goals that align with their deepest desires and aspirations, ensuring that their efforts are focused and purposeful.

Once clarity is established, the next step is to set specific, measurable, achievable, relevant, and time-bound (SMART) goals. Specific goals clearly define what you want to accomplish, why it's important, and how you plan to achieve it. Measurable goals allow you to track your progress and evaluate your success. Achievable goals are realistic and within reach, given your resources, skills, and constraints. Relevant goals align with your values, priorities, and long-term aspirations. Finally, time-bound goals have a clear deadline or timeline, providing a sense of urgency and accountability.

Breaking down larger goals into smaller, actionable steps is another key aspect of effective goal setting. This approach, often referred to as chunking or scaffolding, makes goals more manageable and less overwhelming. By focusing on one step at a time, individuals can build momentum, gain confidence, and make steady progress toward their ultimate objectives. Each small victory serves as motivation to continue moving forward, even when faced with challenges or setbacks.

Accountability and commitment are crucial for achieving goals. Sharing your goals with a trusted friend, family member, or mentor can provide support, encouragement, and accountability. Additionally, publicly committing to your goals, whether through social media, writing them down, or creating a vision board, increases your sense of responsibility and commitment. Regularly reviewing your progress and celebrating your achievements along the way reinforces positive behavior and keeps you motivated.

Flexibility and adaptability are also important qualities when it comes to goal setting. Life is unpredictable, and obstacles and setbacks are inevitable. Instead of viewing challenges as failures, see them as opportunities for growth and learning. Being open to adjusting your goals and strategies as needed allows you to navigate obstacles more effectively and stay on track toward your desired outcomes.

Visualization and positive affirmation techniques can enhance the effectiveness of goal setting. Visualization involves mentally rehearsing achieving your goals, imagining the process and the outcome in vivid detail. Positive affirmations are positive statements that you repeat to yourself to reinforce your belief in your ability to achieve your goals. By visualizing success and affirming your capabilities, you program your subconscious mind for success and increase your confidence and motivation.

In addition to setting outcome goals, it's important to set process goals that focus on the actions and behaviors necessary to achieve your desired outcomes. Process goals are within your control and provide a roadmap for success. For example, if your outcome goal is to lose weight, your process goals might include exercising for 30 minutes each day, eating a balanced diet, and tracking your food intake. By focusing on the process, you can make consistent progress toward your desired outcomes.

Another effective strategy for goal setting is to prioritize your goals and focus on the most important ones first. Not all goals are created equal, and it's important to identify which goals will have the greatest impact on your life and prioritize them accordingly. By focusing your time, energy, and resources on your highest-priority goals, you can maximize your effectiveness and achieve meaningful results.

Finally, it's important to celebrate your achievements and acknowledge your progress along the way. Celebrating small wins boosts your confidence and motivation, reinforces positive behavior, and creates momentum for future success. Whether it's treating yourself to a reward, sharing your achievements with others, or simply taking a moment to reflect on how far you've come, acknowledging your progress is essential for staying motivated and committed to your goals.

Chapter 7: Mindful Living

Mindful living is a transformative approach to life that involves cultivating present-moment awareness, acceptance, and compassion in all aspects of daily existence. In a world filled with distractions, demands, and constant busyness, mindful living offers a pathway to greater peace, clarity, and fulfillment. It involves paying attention to the present moment with openness, curiosity, and non-judgment, and embracing each moment as an opportunity for growth and connection. By integrating mindfulness practices into everyday life, individuals can reduce stress, enhance well-being, and experience greater joy and meaning.

At the core of mindful living is the practice of mindfulness, which involves bringing one's attention to the present moment with openness, curiosity, and acceptance. This means tuning into the sights, sounds, sensations, and thoughts that arise in each moment without judgment or attachment. Mindfulness can be practiced formally through meditation, yoga, or tai chi, or informally through everyday activities such as eating, walking, or even washing dishes.

One of the key benefits of mindful living is its ability to reduce stress and promote relaxation. By bringing attention to the present moment, individuals can break free from the cycle of rumination, worry, and anxiety that often accompanies modern life. Instead of dwelling on the past or fretting about the future, mindfulness allows individuals to anchor themselves in the present moment, where peace and calm can be found.

Mindful living also enhances emotional well-being by fostering greater self-awareness and emotional regulation. By observing thoughts and feelings as they arise without judgment, individuals can develop a greater understanding of their inner experiences and learn to respond to them with kindness and compassion. This self-awareness allows individuals to navigate difficult emotions more effectively and cultivate a greater sense of resilience in the face of challenges.

In addition to reducing stress and enhancing emotional well-being, mindful living can also improve physical health. Research has shown that mindfulness practices such as meditation can lower blood pressure, reduce inflammation, and boost the immune system. By promoting relaxation and reducing the body's stress response, mindfulness can support overall health and well-being.

Mindful living is also associated with greater interpersonal connection and improved relationships. By being fully present with others, listening deeply, and responding with empathy and compassion, individuals can strengthen their connections and foster greater intimacy and understanding. Mindfulness can also help individuals cultivate a greater sense of gratitude and appreciation for the people and experiences in their lives, leading to greater satisfaction and fulfillment in relationships.

Practicing mindful living involves incorporating mindfulness practices into everyday life and cultivating a mindset of presence and awareness. This can include formal practices such as meditation or yoga, as well as informal practices such as mindful eating, walking, or breathing. By bringing attention to the present moment in all activities, individuals can deepen their experience of life and cultivate a greater sense of peace and fulfillment.

One of the key principles of mindful living is acceptance, which involves acknowledging and embracing the present moment as it is, without judgment or resistance. This means accepting both the pleasant and unpleasant aspects of life with equanimity and compassion. By letting go of the need to control or change things, individuals can find greater peace and contentment in the midst of life's ups and downs.

Another important aspect of mindful living is self-compassion, which involves treating oneself with kindness and understanding, especially in times of difficulty or suffering. By cultivating a mindset of self-compassion, individuals can respond to their own struggles with greater empathy and care, leading to greater resilience and well-being.

Mindful living also involves cultivating a greater sense of connection to the world around us. This can include developing a deeper appreciation for the natural world, as well as fostering greater empathy and compassion for all living beings. By recognizing our interconnectedness with all beings and the planet, individuals can cultivate a greater sense of responsibility and stewardship for the world we share.

Incorporating mindfulness into everyday life involves creating moments of stillness and reflection amidst the busyness of daily life. This can be as simple as taking a few deep breaths, pausing to notice the sensations in the body, or bringing awareness to the present moment while performing routine tasks. By incorporating mindfulness into daily routines, individuals can create moments of peace and presence that nourish the mind, body, and spirit.

Mindful living is not about achieving a state of perfection or enlightenment; rather, it is a lifelong journey of self-discovery and growth. By cultivating present-moment awareness, acceptance, and compassion in all aspects of life, individuals can experience greater peace, clarity, and fulfillment, even in the midst of life's challenges and uncertainties. Mindful living offers a pathway to greater well-being and connection, allowing individuals to live more fully and authentically in the present moment.

Chapter 8: Exercise and Movement

Exercise and movement are essential components of a healthy lifestyle, providing numerous physical, mental, and emotional benefits that contribute to overall well-being. Whether it's going for a run, practicing yoga, lifting weights, or simply taking a brisk walk, engaging in regular physical activity is one of the most effective ways to energize the body, improve fitness, and enhance quality of life.

Exercise and movement are vital for maintaining optimal physical health. Regular physical activity strengthens the cardiovascular system, improves circulation, and enhances lung function, reducing the risk of chronic diseases such as heart disease, stroke, and diabetes. Exercise also helps maintain a healthy weight by burning calories and building lean muscle mass, which in turn boosts metabolism and increases energy levels.

Engaging in regular exercise has numerous benefits for mental health and emotional well-being. Physical activity stimulates the production of endorphins, neurotransmitters that promote feelings of happiness and euphoria, leading to a reduction in stress, anxiety, and depression. Exercise also improves cognitive function, memory, and concentration, enhancing overall mental clarity and performance.

Furthermore, exercise and movement play a crucial role in promoting longevity and healthy aging. Regular physical activity has been shown to increase lifespan and reduce the risk of age-related diseases such as Alzheimer's disease, osteoporosis, and certain types of cancer. Exercise also helps maintain mobility, flexibility, and balance, reducing the risk of falls and injuries in older adults.

There are many different types of exercise and movement, each offering unique benefits and catering to different preferences, fitness levels, and goals. Aerobic exercise, such as running, cycling, and swimming, improves cardiovascular fitness, endurance, and stamina, while also burning calories and promoting weight loss. Strength training, which involves lifting weights or using resistance bands, builds muscle strength and tone, increases metabolism, and enhances overall physical performance.

Flexibility exercises, such as yoga and stretching, improve range of motion, reduce muscle tension, and prevent injury by increasing flexibility and mobility. Balance exercises, such as tai chi and Pilates, improve stability, coordination, and proprioception, reducing the risk of falls and enhancing overall physical function.

Incorporating a variety of exercises into your routine is important for achieving a balanced and well-rounded fitness program. Cross-training, which involves alternating between different types of exercise, helps prevent boredom, reduces the risk of overuse injuries, and maximizes overall fitness gains. Mixing up your workouts also keeps your body challenged and prevents plateaus in performance.

Creating a personalized exercise plan involves setting specific goals, identifying activities you enjoy, and considering your fitness level, schedule, and preferences. Start by setting SMART goals—specific, measurable, achievable, relevant, and time-bound—that are tailored to your individual needs and aspirations. Whether your goal is to lose weight, build muscle, improve flexibility, or increase endurance, having a clear plan in place will help keep you motivated and focused.

When designing your exercise routine, consider incorporating a combination of cardiovascular exercise, strength training, flexibility exercises, and balance training to achieve comprehensive fitness results. Aim for at least 150 minutes of moderate-intensity aerobic activity or 75 minutes of vigorous-intensity aerobic activity per week, along with two or more days of strength training exercises targeting all major muscle groups.

Consistency is key when it comes to reaping the benefits of exercise and movement. Schedule your workouts at times that work best for your schedule and make them a priority in your daily routine. Find activities that you enjoy and look forward to, whether it's taking a dance class, going for a hike, or practicing martial arts. Having fun and enjoying the process will help keep you motivated and committed to your fitness goals.

In addition to structured exercise, it's important to incorporate movement into your daily life by staying active throughout the day. Take the stairs instead of the elevator, walk or bike to work if possible, and incorporate short bursts of activity into your day, such as doing squats while brushing your teeth or taking a brisk walk during your lunch break. Every little bit of movement adds up and contributes to your overall health and well-being.

Listening to your body and practicing self-care are important aspects of maintaining a safe and sustainable exercise routine. Pay attention to how your body feels during and after exercise, and adjust your intensity, duration, and frequency accordingly. Rest and recovery are essential for preventing overtraining and injury, so be sure to incorporate rest days into your schedule and prioritize sleep, hydration, and nutrition to support your body's recovery process.

Chapter 9: Healthy Eating

Healthy eating is a fundamental aspect of overall well-being, encompassing not only the physical nourishment of the body but also the emotional and spiritual nourishment of the soul. It involves making conscious and mindful choices about the foods we consume, prioritizing nutrient-dense whole foods, and cultivating a positive relationship with food and eating. Healthy eating is not about restriction or deprivation but rather about nourishing the body and soul with foods that promote health, vitality, and balance.

The importance of healthy eating cannot be overstated. Proper nutrition is essential for supporting the body's growth, development, and maintenance of optimal health. A well-balanced diet provides the necessary nutrients, vitamins, minerals, and antioxidants that support immune function, promote healthy digestion, and reduce the risk of chronic diseases such as heart disease, diabetes, and cancer. Healthy eating also supports mental and emotional well-being, providing the energy and nutrients needed for cognitive function, mood regulation, and overall mental clarity and vitality.

In addition to its physical benefits, healthy eating also plays a crucial role in nourishing the soul. Food is not only fuel for the body but also a source of pleasure, enjoyment, and connection. Sharing meals with loved ones, savoring delicious flavors and textures, and exploring new culinary experiences can bring joy and fulfillment to our lives. By approaching food with mindfulness, gratitude, and appreciation, we can cultivate a deeper connection to ourselves, others, and the world around us.

At the heart of healthy eating is a focus on whole, minimally processed foods that are as close to their natural state as possible. This includes a variety of fruits, vegetables, whole grains, lean proteins, and healthy fats, as well as plenty of water and herbal teas. These foods are rich in vitamins, minerals, fiber, and antioxidants, and provide the essential nutrients needed for optimal health and vitality.

One of the key principles of healthy eating is balance and moderation. Rather than adhering to strict rules or fad diets, healthy eating involves finding a sustainable and enjoyable way of eating that works for your individual needs and preferences. This may include incorporating a variety of foods from all food groups, enjoying treats and indulgences in moderation, and listening to your body's hunger and fullness cues.

Another important aspect of healthy eating is mindfulness. Mindful eating involves paying attention to the sensory experience of eating, including the taste, texture, and aroma of food, as well as the physical sensations of hunger and fullness. By tuning into our body's signals and eating with awareness, we can cultivate a greater appreciation for food and make more conscious choices about what and how much we eat.

Incorporating healthy eating into daily life involves planning and preparation. This may include meal planning, grocery shopping, and food preparation to ensure that nutritious options are readily available and convenient. Stocking your kitchen with healthy staples such as fruits, vegetables, whole grains, and lean proteins makes it easier to make nutritious choices throughout the week.

In addition to focusing on whole foods, it's also important to pay attention to portion sizes and eating patterns. Eating mindfully and stopping when you're satisfied helps prevent overeating and promotes a healthy relationship with food. It's also important to listen to your body's hunger and fullness cues and eat in response to physical hunger rather than emotional or external cues.

Healthy eating is not just about what you eat but also how you eat. Taking the time to sit down and eat without distractions, such as television or electronic devices, allows you to fully savor and enjoy your food. Chewing slowly and mindfully and paying attention to the flavors and textures of each bite helps you feel more satisfied and prevents overeating.

Chapter 10: Sleep Hygiene

Sleep hygiene refers to a set of practices and habits that promote quality sleep and overall well-being. It involves creating a sleep-friendly environment, establishing a regular sleep schedule, and adopting behaviors that support restorative sleep. Good sleep hygiene is essential for physical health, mental clarity, emotional well-being, and optimal performance in all areas of life.

Quality sleep is essential for overall health and well-being. During sleep, the body undergoes important processes that support physical repair, immune function, hormone regulation, and cognitive function. Adequate sleep is also crucial for memory consolidation, learning, and emotional regulation. By prioritizing good sleep hygiene, individuals can improve their physical health, mental clarity, and emotional resilience, leading to greater overall well-being and success in all areas of life.

One of the key principles of good sleep hygiene is maintaining a consistent sleep schedule. Going to bed and waking up at the same time every day helps regulate the body's internal clock, or circadian rhythm, promoting more restful and refreshing sleep. Consistency is important not only on weekdays but also on weekends, as irregular sleep patterns can disrupt the body's natural sleep-wake cycle and lead to difficulty falling asleep or staying asleep.

Creating a sleep-friendly environment is another important aspect of good sleep hygiene. This involves optimizing the bedroom for rest and relaxation by minimizing noise, light, and temperature disruptions. Keeping the bedroom dark, quiet, and cool can promote deeper and more restorative sleep. Additionally, investing in a comfortable mattress, pillows, and bedding that provide adequate support and comfort can enhance sleep quality and duration.

Establishing a relaxing bedtime routine can help signal to the body that it's time to wind down and prepare for sleep. This may include activities such as taking a warm bath, practicing relaxation techniques such as deep breathing or meditation, or reading a book. Engaging in calming activities before bed can help reduce stress and anxiety, making it easier to fall asleep and stay asleep throughout the night.

Limiting exposure to screens and electronic devices before bed is important for promoting restful sleep. The blue light emitted by smartphones, tablets, computers, and televisions can disrupt the body's production of melatonin, a hormone that regulates sleep-wake cycles. Limiting screen time in the hour before bed and using devices with a blue light filter can help mitigate the effects of blue light on sleep quality.

Managing stress and anxiety is also important for improving sleep quality. Stress and anxiety can interfere with the body's ability to relax and fall asleep, leading to difficulty sleeping and poor sleep quality. Practicing relaxation techniques such as deep breathing, progressive muscle relaxation, or meditation can help reduce stress and promote feelings of calm and relaxation, making it easier to fall asleep and stay asleep throughout the night.

Avoiding stimulants such as caffeine, nicotine, and alcohol close to bedtime is important for promoting restful sleep. These substances can disrupt the body's natural sleep-wake cycle and interfere with the quality and duration of sleep. Limiting caffeine intake to the morning hours and avoiding alcohol and nicotine in the evening can help promote better sleep quality and overall well-being.

Incorporating regular physical activity into your daily routine can also improve sleep quality. Exercise helps reduce stress, anxiety, and tension, making it easier to fall asleep and stay asleep throughout the night. However, it's important to avoid vigorous exercise close to bedtime, as it can have a stimulating effect on the body and make it harder to wind down and relax before bed.

Evaluating and addressing any underlying sleep disorders or medical conditions is essential for improving sleep quality. Conditions such as sleep apnea, insomnia, restless legs syndrome, and narcolepsy can disrupt sleep and lead to daytime fatigue and impaired cognitive function. Seeking medical evaluation and treatment for sleep disorders can help identify and address underlying issues that may be contributing to poor sleep quality.

Chapter 11: Stress Management

Stress management is a multifaceted approach to coping with the challenges and demands of everyday life in a healthy and effective manner. It involves recognizing the sources of stress, implementing strategies to reduce its impact, and cultivating resilience to navigate life's ups and downs with greater ease and balance. In today's fast-paced and interconnected world, stress has become a common experience for many people, but learning how to manage it can lead to improved physical health, mental well-being, and overall quality of life.

The importance of stress management cannot be overstated. Chronic stress has been linked to a wide range of physical and mental health problems, including heart disease, hypertension, diabetes, depression, anxiety, and insomnia. By learning how to effectively manage stress, individuals can reduce their risk of developing these health problems and improve their overall quality of life. Stress management is also important for enhancing resilience, adaptability, and coping skills, enabling individuals to navigate life's challenges with greater ease and grace.

One of the key principles of stress management is identifying the sources of stress in your life. This may include external stressors such as work deadlines, financial pressures, relationship conflicts, or major life changes, as well as internal stressors such as perfectionism, self-criticism, or negative thinking patterns. By becoming aware of the factors that contribute to stress, individuals can begin to take proactive steps to address them and reduce their impact on their physical and mental well-being.

Implementing stress-reduction techniques is another important aspect of stress management. There are many different strategies for reducing stress, and what works for one person may not work for another. Some common stress-reduction techniques include mindfulness meditation, deep breathing exercises, progressive muscle relaxation, yoga, tai chi, and guided imagery. These techniques help activate the body's relaxation response, reduce muscle tension, lower blood pressure and heart rate, and promote feelings of calm and relaxation.

Physical activity is also an effective stress management tool. Exercise helps release endorphins, neurotransmitters that act as natural painkillers and mood elevators, reducing feelings of stress and anxiety. Regular physical activity also improves cardiovascular health, boosts immune function, and enhances overall well-being. Whether it's going for a walk, practicing yoga, or hitting the gym, finding ways to incorporate movement into your daily routine can have a profound impact on your ability to manage stress.

In addition to practicing stress-reduction techniques and engaging in regular physical activity, it's also important to cultivate healthy lifestyle habits that support overall well-being. This includes eating a balanced diet, getting adequate sleep, staying hydrated, and avoiding excessive caffeine, alcohol, and nicotine. Making time for activities you enjoy, spending time in nature, and nurturing positive relationships with friends and loved ones are also important for reducing stress and promoting emotional well-being.

Learning how to reframe negative thinking patterns and develop a more positive and resilient mindset is another important aspect of stress management. This involves challenging negative beliefs and assumptions, practicing self-compassion and self-care, and cultivating gratitude and optimism. By focusing on the present moment, adopting a growth mindset, and embracing uncertainty and change as opportunities for growth and learning, individuals can develop greater resilience and adaptability in the face of stress.

Effective time management is also crucial for stress management. Many people feel stressed and overwhelmed because they have too much on their plate and not enough time to get everything done. By prioritizing tasks, setting realistic goals, and learning how to say no to non-essential commitments, individuals can reduce feelings of overwhelm and create a greater sense of balance and control in their lives.

Finally, seeking support from others is an important aspect of stress management. Talking to friends, family members, or a trusted counselor or therapist can provide validation, perspective, and emotional support during difficult times. Support groups and community organizations can also offer valuable resources and connections for individuals dealing with specific stressors or challenges.

Chapter 12: Productivity Hacks

Productivity hacks are strategies, techniques, and tools that individuals can use to optimize their efficiency, manage their time effectively, and accomplish more in less time. In today's fast-paced and demanding world, the ability to maximize productivity is essential for achieving personal and professional goals, reducing stress, and maintaining a healthy work-life balance. Productivity hacks encompass a wide range of approaches, from time management techniques to organizational strategies to mindset shifts, all aimed at helping individuals work smarter, not harder.

The importance of productivity hacks lies in their ability to help individuals overcome common challenges such as procrastination, distraction, and overwhelm, and achieve greater focus, efficiency, and effectiveness in their work. By implementing productivity hacks, individuals can optimize their time and energy, prioritize tasks, and streamline workflows, leading to increased productivity, improved performance, and reduced stress.

One of the key principles of productivity hacks is identifying and prioritizing tasks based on their importance and urgency. This involves using techniques such as the Eisenhower Matrix, which categorizes tasks into four quadrants based on their level of urgency and importance: important and urgent, important but not urgent, urgent but not important, and neither urgent nor important. By focusing on tasks that are both important and urgent, individuals can maximize their impact and avoid getting bogged down by low-priority tasks.

Another important principle of productivity hacks is minimizing distractions and interruptions. This may involve implementing strategies such as time blocking, which involves scheduling specific blocks of time for focused work without interruption, or using productivity tools such as website blockers and notification management apps to limit distractions from email, social media, and other sources. Creating a dedicated workspace free from clutter and distractions can also help promote focus and concentration.

Effective time management is also crucial for maximizing productivity. This may involve using techniques such as the Pomodoro Technique, which involves breaking work into short, focused intervals (typically 25 minutes) followed by short breaks, or the time-blocking method, which involves scheduling specific blocks of time for different tasks or activities. By planning and prioritizing tasks in advance and allocating time for focused work, individuals can make the most of their time and avoid wasting time on unproductive activities.

In addition to time management techniques, organizational strategies are also important for optimizing productivity. This may involve using tools such as to-do lists, task management apps, and project management software to keep track of tasks, deadlines, and projects. Breaking down larger tasks into smaller, more manageable steps and setting deadlines and milestones can also help keep projects on track and prevent overwhelm.

Maintaining a healthy work-life balance is another important aspect of productivity hacks. Burnout and fatigue can negatively impact productivity and overall well-being, so it's important to take breaks, prioritize self-care, and set boundaries between work and personal life. This may involve scheduling regular breaks throughout the day, setting limits on work hours, and making time for hobbies, exercise, and relaxation.

Cultivating a growth mindset is also important for maximizing productivity. Instead of viewing challenges as obstacles, individuals with a growth mindset see them as opportunities for learning and growth. By embracing a positive attitude, seeking feedback, and focusing on continuous improvement, individuals can overcome setbacks and obstacles more effectively and achieve greater success in their personal and professional lives.

Chapter 13: Time Management

Time management is the art and science of effectively organizing and prioritizing one's time to achieve goals, complete tasks efficiently, and maximize productivity. In today's fast-paced world, where demands on our time seem to be constantly increasing, mastering time management skills is essential for success in both personal and professional endeavors. By learning how to make the most of every minute, individuals can reduce stress, increase productivity, and create more time for the things that truly matter.

The importance of time management cannot be overstated. Effective time management is essential for achieving goals, meeting deadlines, and maintaining a healthy work-life balance. By learning how to prioritize tasks, eliminate time-wasting activities, and optimize workflows, individuals can make the most of their time and accomplish more with less stress. Time management skills are also crucial for reducing procrastination, overcoming overwhelm, and maintaining focus and concentration in the face of distractions.

One of the key principles of time management is prioritization. This involves identifying tasks and activities based on their importance and urgency and allocating time and resources accordingly. The Eisenhower Matrix, mentioned earlier in the productivity hacks section, is a useful tool for prioritizing tasks based on their level of urgency and importance. By focusing on tasks that are both important and urgent, individuals can maximize their impact and avoid getting bogged down by low-priority activities.

Effective time management also involves setting clear goals and deadlines. By establishing specific, measurable, achievable, relevant, and time-bound (SMART) goals, individuals can create a roadmap for success and stay motivated and focused on their objectives. Breaking down larger goals into smaller, more manageable tasks and setting deadlines and milestones can help keep projects on track and prevent procrastination.

Another important aspect of time management is planning and scheduling. This involves allocating time for different tasks and activities, creating to-do lists, and using calendars or planners to organize deadlines and appointments. Time blocking, mentioned earlier in the productivity hacks section, is a useful technique for scheduling specific blocks of time for focused work without interruption. By planning and prioritizing tasks in advance, individuals can make the most of their time and avoid wasting time on unproductive activities.

Minimizing distractions and interruptions is also crucial for effective time management. This may involve implementing strategies such as setting boundaries with coworkers or family members, turning off notifications on electronic devices, and creating a dedicated workspace free from clutter and distractions. Using productivity tools such as website blockers and time-tracking apps can also help limit distractions and promote focus and concentration.

Effective delegation is another important time management skill. Delegating tasks to others can help free up time for more important or higher-priority activities and reduce the risk of burnout and overwhelm. It's important to delegate tasks based on each person's strengths and skills and provide clear instructions and expectations to ensure successful outcomes.

Maintaining a healthy work-life balance is also essential for effective time management. Burnout and fatigue can negatively impact productivity and overall well-being, so it's important to make time for rest, relaxation, and self-care. This may involve scheduling regular breaks throughout the day, setting limits on work hours, and making time for hobbies, exercise, and time spent with loved ones.

Chapter 14: Building Resilience

Building resilience is the process of adapting and bouncing back from adversity, challenges, and setbacks. It involves developing the capacity to withstand and overcome difficult experiences, while also growing stronger and more resilient in the face of adversity. Resilience is not a fixed trait; it can be cultivated and strengthened over time through intentional practice and the adoption of specific mindset and behavioral strategies. In today's unpredictable and rapidly changing world, resilience is a valuable skill that can help individuals navigate life's ups and downs with greater ease, adaptability, and optimism.

The importance of building resilience cannot be overstated. Resilience is essential for coping with the inevitable challenges and setbacks that life throws our way, whether they are personal, professional, or global in nature. By developing resilience, individuals can bounce back from adversity more quickly and effectively, maintain a positive outlook in the face of difficulties, and emerge stronger and more resourceful than before. Resilience is also associated with greater mental and emotional well-being, improved stress management skills, and increased overall life satisfaction.

One of the key principles of building resilience is cultivating a growth mindset. A growth mindset is the belief that abilities and intelligence can be developed through effort, practice, and perseverance. Individuals with a growth mindset view challenges and setbacks as opportunities for learning and growth, rather than insurmountable obstacles. By embracing a growth mindset, individuals can approach adversity with resilience, optimism, and a sense of possibility, rather than fear or defeat.

Another important aspect of building resilience is developing strong social support networks. Social support from friends, family members, colleagues, and community members can provide emotional validation, encouragement, and practical assistance during difficult times. Cultivating strong social connections, maintaining open lines of communication, and seeking support from others when needed can help individuals cope with stress and adversity more effectively and build resilience.

Practicing self-care and prioritizing physical and emotional well-being are also essential for building resilience. This may involve engaging in activities that promote relaxation and stress relief, such as meditation, mindfulness, yoga, or spending time in nature. Getting regular exercise, eating a balanced diet, and getting enough sleep are also important for maintaining physical health and resilience. Taking time for hobbies, interests, and activities that bring joy and fulfillment can also help replenish energy and build resilience.

Developing problem-solving and coping skills is another important aspect of building resilience. This may involve breaking problems down into smaller, more manageable steps, brainstorming potential solutions, and seeking help or guidance when needed. Learning to regulate emotions, manage stress, and practice self-compassion are also important for coping with adversity and building resilience. Developing a toolkit of coping strategies, such as deep breathing exercises, progressive muscle relaxation, or positive self-talk, can help individuals navigate difficult emotions and situations with greater ease and resilience.

Fostering a sense of purpose and meaning in life is also important for building resilience. Having a sense of purpose and direction can provide motivation and resilience during difficult times, helping individuals stay focused on their goals and values, even in the face of adversity. Cultivating gratitude, practicing acts of kindness, and finding meaning in challenges and setbacks can help individuals build resilience and maintain a positive outlook on life.

Finally, practicing flexibility and adaptability is essential for building resilience. Life is unpredictable, and setbacks and challenges are inevitable. Learning to adapt to change, adjust expectations, and find creative solutions to problems can help individuals navigate uncertainty with greater ease and resilience. Embracing uncertainty as a natural part of life and focusing on what can be controlled, rather than dwelling on what cannot, can help individuals build resilience and thrive in the face of adversity.

Chapter 15: Gratitude Practice

Gratitude practice is the intentional and regular expression of appreciation for the positive aspects of life, both big and small. It involves consciously focusing on the blessings, joys, and gifts in one's life, and expressing gratitude for them through words, actions, or thoughts. Cultivating a grateful heart has been associated with numerous physical, mental, and emotional benefits, including increased happiness, improved relationships, reduced stress, and enhanced overall well-being.

The importance of gratitude practice lies in its transformative power to shift one's perspective from focusing on what's lacking or negative to recognizing and appreciating the abundance and goodness that already exists in life. In today's fast-paced and often stressful world, it's easy to overlook the simple pleasures and blessings that surround us each day. By practicing gratitude, individuals can cultivate a more positive and optimistic outlook on life, leading to greater resilience, contentment, and fulfillment.

One of the key principles of gratitude practice is mindfulness. Mindfulness involves paying attention to the present moment with openness, curiosity, and acceptance. By cultivating awareness of the present moment and intentionally focusing on the positive aspects of life, individuals can cultivate gratitude and appreciation for the here and now. Mindful gratitude practice involves tuning into the sights, sounds, smells, tastes, and sensations of everyday life, and acknowledging the beauty and wonder that surrounds us.

Another important aspect of gratitude practice is keeping a gratitude journal. A gratitude journal is a simple and effective tool for cultivating gratitude and appreciation. Each day, individuals can take a few minutes to write down three to five things they're grateful for, whether it's a beautiful sunrise, a kind gesture from a friend, or a moment of laughter with loved ones. Reflecting on the positive aspects of life and documenting them in a gratitude journal can help shift focus away from negativity and cultivate a more positive mindset.

Practicing gratitude in relationships is also important for cultivating a thankful heart. Expressing gratitude to loved ones for their kindness, support, and presence can strengthen bonds and deepen connections. Whether it's saying thank you, writing a heartfelt note, or performing acts of kindness, expressing gratitude to others not only benefits them but also enhances one's own sense of well-being and satisfaction.

In addition to expressing gratitude to others, it's also important to cultivate self-gratitude. Self-gratitude involves acknowledging and appreciating one's own strengths, accomplishments, and qualities. This may involve celebrating small victories, recognizing personal growth and progress, and practicing self-compassion and self-care. Cultivating self-gratitude can help build self-esteem, resilience, and a sense of worthiness, leading to greater overall well-being and happiness.

Practicing gratitude rituals and routines can also help cultivate a thankful heart. This may involve starting or ending each day with a moment of gratitude, incorporating gratitude into daily meditation or prayer practices, or creating gratitude rituals such as keeping a gratitude jar or setting aside time each week to reflect on blessings and accomplishments. By making gratitude a regular part of one's routine, individuals can cultivate a more grateful and appreciative mindset over time.

Finally, cultivating a sense of awe and wonder is an important aspect of gratitude practice. Awe involves experiencing a sense of wonder, reverence, and appreciation for the beauty and majesty of the world around us. Whether it's witnessing a breathtaking sunset, marveling at the grandeur of nature, or contemplating the mysteries of the universe, cultivating awe can inspire feelings of gratitude and humility, and deepen one's appreciation for the richness and complexity of life.

Chapter 16: Positive Thinking

Positive thinking is a mindset and cognitive approach that involves consciously directing one's thoughts and inner dialogue towards optimistic, constructive, and empowering perspectives. It entails focusing on the bright side of situations, looking for opportunities in challenges, and reframing negative thoughts into more positive and affirming ones. Positive thinking is not about ignoring or denying reality; rather, it's about choosing to interpret events and circumstances in a way that fosters resilience, growth, and well-being.

The importance of positive thinking lies in its profound impact on mental, emotional, and physical well-being. Research has shown that cultivating a positive mindset can lead to numerous benefits, including increased resilience, improved stress management skills, enhanced immune function, and greater overall life satisfaction. By transforming negative thought patterns and cultivating more positive and optimistic perspectives, individuals can improve their quality of life and enhance their ability to cope with adversity and challenges.

One of the key principles of positive thinking is awareness of thought patterns. Many people are unaware of the constant stream of thoughts that run through their minds each day. By becoming more mindful of one's thoughts and inner dialogue, individuals can begin to identify patterns of negativity, self-criticism, and pessimism, and take steps to challenge and change them. Mindfulness practices such as meditation, deep breathing, and body scan exercises can help cultivate awareness of thought patterns and promote a more positive mindset.

Another important aspect of positive thinking is reframing negative thoughts. Reframing involves consciously challenging and changing negative interpretations of events and circumstances into more positive and empowering ones. For example, instead of viewing a setback as a failure, one might reframe it as an opportunity for growth and learning. By reframing negative thoughts into more positive and constructive ones, individuals can shift their perspective and cultivate a greater sense of optimism and resilience.

Practicing gratitude is also an essential aspect of positive thinking. Gratitude involves focusing on the blessings, joys, and gifts in one's life, and expressing appreciation for them. By cultivating a mindset of gratitude, individuals can shift their focus away from what's lacking or negative and towards what's abundant and positive. Gratitude practices such as keeping a gratitude journal, expressing appreciation to others, and practicing mindful gratitude can help cultivate a more positive and optimistic outlook on life.

Cultivating self-compassion is another important aspect of positive thinking. Self-compassion involves treating oneself with kindness, understanding, and acceptance, especially in the face of difficulties or setbacks. Instead of harsh self-criticism and judgment, individuals with self-compassion respond to themselves with warmth and understanding, acknowledging their humanity and inherent worthiness. Cultivating self-compassion can help individuals challenge negative thought patterns and develop a more positive and supportive inner dialogue.

Practicing positive affirmations is a powerful tool for transforming inner dialogue and cultivating a positive mindset. Positive affirmations are statements that affirm positive qualities, beliefs, and intentions, and are repeated regularly to reinforce positive thought patterns. Examples of positive affirmations include "I am worthy and deserving of love and happiness," "I believe in my abilities to overcome challenges," and "I am resilient and capable of handling whatever comes my way." By repeating positive affirmations regularly, individuals can reprogram their subconscious mind and cultivate a more positive and empowering inner dialogue.

Surrounding oneself with positivity is also important for fostering positive thinking. This may involve seeking out uplifting and inspiring sources of information, such as books, podcasts, and social media accounts that promote positivity and personal growth. Spending time with supportive and encouraging friends and family members can also help reinforce positive thought patterns and cultivate a more optimistic outlook on life.

Chapter 17: Self-Care Strategies

Self-care strategies are intentional practices and activities that individuals engage in to promote their physical, mental, and emotional well-being. These strategies involve taking proactive steps to nurture and care for oneself, prioritizing personal needs and boundaries, and fostering a sense of balance, resilience, and vitality in daily life. In today's fast-paced and demanding world, self-care is essential for maintaining health, happiness, and overall quality of life.

The importance of self-care strategies lies in their ability to replenish energy, reduce stress, and enhance overall well-being. Self-care is not selfish; it's a vital component of maintaining health and happiness, and it enables individuals to show up as their best selves in all areas of life. By prioritizing self-care, individuals can prevent burnout, improve resilience, and cultivate a greater sense of balance, fulfillment, and vitality.

One of the key principles of self-care strategies is recognizing and honoring personal needs and boundaries. This involves tuning into one's own physical, mental, and emotional signals and responding to them with compassion and care. It's important to identify and prioritize activities that nourish and replenish energy, whether it's getting enough sleep, eating nutritious foods, engaging in regular exercise, or spending time in nature. Setting and enforcing boundaries with others is also crucial for protecting one's well-being and preventing overwhelm and burnout.

Another important aspect of self-care strategies is cultivating self-awareness and mindfulness. Self-awareness involves paying attention to one's thoughts, feelings, and sensations without judgment, and recognizing when self-care is needed. Mindfulness practices such as meditation, deep breathing, and body scan exercises can help cultivate awareness of internal experiences and promote a greater sense of calm, clarity, and presence in daily life.

Practicing self-compassion is also essential for effective self-care. Self-compassion involves treating oneself with kindness, understanding, and acceptance, especially during times of difficulty or struggle. Instead of harsh self-criticism and judgment, individuals with self-compassion respond to themselves with warmth and understanding, acknowledging their humanity and inherent worthiness. Cultivating self-compassion can help individuals navigate challenges with greater resilience and self-care, and foster a greater sense of well-being and self-worth.

Creating a self-care routine is another important aspect of self-care strategies. A self-care routine is a set of practices and activities that individuals engage in regularly to promote their physical, mental, and emotional well-being. This may include activities such as exercise, meditation, journaling, creative expression, hobbies, or spending time with loved ones. By prioritizing self-care and making it a regular part of daily life, individuals can maintain balance, reduce stress, and enhance overall well-being.

In addition to regular self-care practices, it's also important to incorporate self-care into daily life through small, everyday acts of kindness and self-compassion. This may include taking short breaks throughout the day to rest and recharge, practicing deep breathing or mindfulness exercises during stressful moments, or engaging in activities that bring joy and pleasure. By incorporating self-care into daily life in small, manageable ways, individuals can cultivate a greater sense of well-being and resilience over time.

Seeking support from others is also important for effective self-care. Whether it's reaching out to friends, family members, or a therapist or counselor, seeking support can provide validation, encouragement, and guidance during difficult times. Support groups and community organizations can also offer valuable resources and connections for individuals seeking to prioritize their well-being and engage in self-care practices.

Chapter 18: Building Strong Relationships

Building strong relationships is a multifaceted process that involves forming meaningful connections with others, nurturing trust and intimacy, and fostering mutual respect, support, and understanding. Strong relationships are essential for overall well-being and happiness, as they provide a sense of belonging, connection, and support, and contribute to physical, mental, and emotional health. In today's interconnected world, building and maintaining strong relationships is more important than ever, as they play a crucial role in navigating life's challenges, celebrating successes, and finding fulfillment and meaning.

The importance of building strong relationships cannot be overstated. Strong relationships provide a sense of belonging and connection, which are fundamental human needs. Research has shown that people with strong social connections are happier, healthier, and live longer lives than those who are socially isolated. Strong relationships also provide emotional support during difficult times, enhance resilience, and contribute to greater overall life satisfaction and well-being.

One of the key principles of building strong relationships is effective communication. Communication is the foundation of any healthy relationship, and involves both speaking and listening with openness, honesty, and empathy. Effective communication requires active listening, validation of feelings, and clear and respectful expression of thoughts and emotions. By communicating openly and honestly with others, individuals can build trust, resolve conflicts, and deepen connections.

Another important aspect of building strong relationships is fostering mutual respect and understanding. Strong relationships are built on a foundation of mutual respect, where each person's thoughts, feelings, and boundaries are valued and honored. This involves recognizing and appreciating differences, being open to new perspectives, and treating others with kindness, compassion, and empathy. By fostering mutual respect and understanding, individuals can create an environment of trust and safety where relationships can flourish.

Building trust is also essential for strong relationships. Trust is the belief that others will act with integrity, honesty, and reliability, and is crucial for establishing and maintaining healthy relationships. Trust is built through consistency, reliability, and transparency in words and actions. By demonstrating trustworthiness and integrity in relationships, individuals can create a solid foundation of trust that enables deeper connection and intimacy.

Nurturing emotional intimacy is another important aspect of building strong relationships. Emotional intimacy involves sharing thoughts, feelings, and vulnerabilities with others in a safe and supportive environment. This requires vulnerability, authenticity, and empathy, as well as a willingness to listen and validate others' experiences. By nurturing emotional intimacy in relationships, individuals can deepen connections, strengthen bonds, and create a sense of closeness and connection.

Investing time and effort into relationships is also crucial for building strong connections with others. Strong relationships require ongoing maintenance and nurturing, including spending quality time together, engaging in meaningful conversations, and participating in shared activities and experiences. By investing time and effort into relationships, individuals can strengthen bonds, build trust, and create lasting connections with others.

Practicing forgiveness and compassion is also important for building strong relationships. Conflict and disagreements are inevitable in any relationship, but how they are handled can determine the strength and longevity of the relationship. Practicing forgiveness involves letting go of resentments and grudges, and extending compassion and understanding to others. By practicing forgiveness and compassion, individuals can repair trust, resolve conflicts, and strengthen relationships.

Finally, maintaining healthy boundaries is essential for building strong relationships. Boundaries are guidelines that define acceptable behavior and interactions in relationships, and help protect individuals' physical, emotional, and psychological well-being. Healthy boundaries involve assertively communicating one's needs and limits, and respecting others' boundaries as well. By maintaining healthy boundaries, individuals can create a sense of safety and respect in relationships, and foster mutual trust and understanding.

Chapter 19: The Power of Saying No

The power of saying no is rooted in the ability to set boundaries and prioritize one's own needs, values, and well-being. Saying no is not only about declining requests or opportunities; it's about asserting oneself, preserving time and energy for what truly matters, and maintaining personal integrity and authenticity. Setting boundaries through the power of saying no is crucial for maintaining healthy relationships, reducing stress, and fostering self-respect and empowerment.

The importance of the power of saying no lies in its ability to protect personal boundaries, values, and priorities. In today's fast-paced and demanding world, it's easy to become overwhelmed by obligations, commitments, and expectations from others. Saying no allows individuals to take control of their time and energy, and to make choices that align with their own needs and values, rather than succumbing to external pressures or people-pleasing tendencies.

One of the key principles of the power of saying no is recognizing and honoring personal limits and boundaries. Boundaries are guidelines that define acceptable behavior and interactions in relationships, and help protect individuals' physical, emotional, and psychological well-being. Saying no is a way of assertively communicating one's boundaries and limits, and asserting oneself in situations where one's needs or values are at risk of being compromised.

Another important aspect of the power of saying no is cultivating self-awareness and self-compassion. Knowing one's own needs, values, and priorities is essential for setting boundaries effectively and saying no with confidence and conviction. It's important to recognize when saying yes to others comes at the expense of one's own well-being, and to prioritize self-care and self-respect by saying no when necessary. Practicing self-compassion involves treating oneself with kindness, understanding, and acceptance, especially when saying no may result in disappointment or disapproval from others.

Building assertiveness skills is also crucial for harnessing the power of saying no. Assertiveness involves expressing one's thoughts, feelings, and needs in a clear, direct, and respectful manner, while also respecting the rights and boundaries of others. Assertive communication allows individuals to say no with confidence and assert their boundaries without feeling guilty or apologizing for their needs. By practicing assertiveness, individuals can strengthen their self-esteem and self-confidence, and build healthier, more authentic relationships based on mutual respect and understanding.

Understanding the difference between assertiveness and aggression is important for effectively harnessing the power of saying no. While assertiveness involves expressing oneself in a direct and respectful manner, aggression involves asserting one's needs at the expense of others, using intimidation or manipulation to get one's way. It's important to assert oneself in a way that respects the rights and boundaries of others and promotes mutual understanding and cooperation.

Practicing self-care and prioritizing well-being is another important aspect of the power of saying no. Saying no allows individuals to preserve time and energy for activities and relationships that nourish and replenish them, rather than deplete them. Prioritizing self-care involves setting aside time for rest, relaxation, and activities that bring joy and fulfillment, and saying no to obligations or commitments that interfere with these priorities. By prioritizing well-being and setting boundaries, individuals can cultivate greater resilience, happiness, and overall life satisfaction.

It's also important to recognize that saying no is a skill that can be learned and practiced over time. For many people, saying no can be difficult due to fear of conflict, rejection, or disappointing others. However, with practice and persistence, individuals can become more comfortable asserting themselves and setting boundaries in a way that feels authentic and respectful. It's okay to start small and gradually work up to saying no in more challenging situations, and to seek support from friends, family members, or a therapist if needed.

Chapter 20: Financial Wellness

Financial wellness encompasses the state of one's overall financial health and well-being, which includes having a stable financial situation, being able to meet financial goals, managing financial stress effectively, and feeling confident and empowered about financial decisions. It's not just about the amount of money one has, but also about how that money is managed and how it impacts overall quality of life. Achieving financial wellness requires creating and maintaining healthy money habits, making informed financial decisions, and developing a positive relationship with money.

The importance of financial wellness cannot be overstated. Financial wellness is closely tied to overall well-being and quality of life, as financial stress can negatively impact physical health, mental health, and relationships. Achieving financial wellness provides a sense of security and stability, reduces anxiety and stress related to money, and allows individuals to pursue their goals and dreams with confidence. By creating healthy money habits and practicing financial wellness, individuals can build a strong foundation for long-term financial security and peace of mind.

One of the key principles of financial wellness is understanding and managing finances effectively. This involves having a clear understanding of one's income, expenses, assets, and liabilities, and making informed decisions about budgeting, saving, investing, and debt management. Understanding basic financial concepts such as budgeting, saving, investing, and credit can help individuals make sound financial decisions and avoid common pitfalls that can lead to financial stress and instability.

Another important aspect of financial wellness is budgeting and financial planning. Budgeting involves creating a plan for how income will be allocated to cover expenses, savings, and debt payments. A budget helps individuals track their spending, identify areas where they can save money, and prioritize financial goals. Financial planning involves setting specific, measurable, achievable, relevant, and time-bound (SMART) financial goals, and developing a plan for achieving them. By budgeting and financial planning, individuals can take control of their finances and work towards their financial goals with confidence.

Building an emergency fund is also essential for financial wellness. An emergency fund is a savings account specifically designated for unexpected expenses or emergencies, such as medical bills, car repairs, or job loss. Having an emergency fund provides a financial safety net and reduces the need to rely on credit cards or loans in times of crisis. Financial experts recommend saving three to six months' worth of living expenses in an emergency fund to provide adequate protection against unforeseen circumstances.

Managing debt effectively is another important aspect of financial wellness. Debt can be a significant source of financial stress and can hinder progress towards financial goals. Developing a plan for paying off debt, prioritizing high-interest debt first, and avoiding taking on new debt whenever possible can help individuals regain control of their finances and achieve greater financial stability. Strategies such as debt consolidation, negotiation with creditors, and refinancing can also help individuals manage debt more effectively and reduce interest payments over time.

Investing for the future is another key component of financial wellness. Investing involves putting money into assets such as stocks, bonds, mutual funds, or real estate with the expectation of generating a return or profit over time. Investing allows individuals to grow their wealth, build long-term financial security, and achieve financial goals such as retirement, education, or homeownership. It's important to develop an investment strategy that aligns with one's financial goals, risk tolerance, and time horizon, and to regularly review and adjust the investment portfolio as needed.

Protecting against financial risks is also important for financial wellness. This may involve purchasing insurance policies such as health insurance, life insurance, disability insurance, and property and casualty insurance to protect against unexpected expenses or loss of income due to illness, injury, or disaster. Having adequate insurance coverage provides financial security and peace of mind, and reduces the risk of financial hardship in the event of unforeseen circumstances.

In addition to managing finances effectively, it's also important to cultivate a positive mindset and attitude towards money. Developing a healthy relationship with money involves understanding one's beliefs, attitudes, and behaviors related to money, and identifying and challenging any negative or limiting beliefs that may be holding one back from achieving financial wellness. Cultivating gratitude, contentment, and generosity can also help individuals develop a more positive and empowering relationship with money, and foster greater overall well-being and happiness.

Chapter 21: Lifelong Learning

Lifelong learning is the ongoing process of acquiring knowledge, skills, and experiences throughout one's entire life. It involves a commitment to personal and professional growth, curiosity, and a desire to explore new ideas and perspectives. Lifelong learning goes beyond formal education and encompasses a wide range of learning opportunities, including self-directed study, workshops, seminars, online courses, and experiential learning. Embracing lifelong learning is essential for staying relevant in a rapidly changing world, adapting to new challenges and opportunities, and fostering personal development and fulfillment.

The importance of lifelong learning cannot be overstated. In today's fast-paced and dynamic world, the pace of change is accelerating, and new technologies, ideas, and opportunities emerge constantly. Lifelong learning is essential for staying informed, adaptable, and competitive in the workforce, as well as for maintaining mental acuity and cognitive function as we age. Lifelong learning also fosters personal growth, creativity, and curiosity, and provides a sense of purpose and fulfillment throughout life.

One of the key principles of lifelong learning is a growth mindset. A growth mindset is the belief that abilities and intelligence can be developed through dedication and hard work. Individuals with a growth mindset embrace challenges, persist in the face of setbacks, and see failures as opportunities for learning and growth. Cultivating a growth mindset is essential for embracing lifelong learning, as it fosters resilience, curiosity, and a passion for continuous improvement.

Another important aspect of lifelong learning is self-directed learning. Self-directed learning involves taking initiative and responsibility for one's own learning, rather than relying solely on formal education or instruction. It allows individuals to pursue their interests, passions, and goals at their own pace and on their own terms.

Self-directed learning may involve reading books, taking online courses, attending workshops or seminars, or engaging in hands-on projects and experiences. By taking ownership of their learning journey, individuals can tailor their learning experiences to their unique needs, interests, and aspirations.

Building a learning mindset is also crucial for embracing lifelong learning. A learning mindset involves approaching life with curiosity, openness, and a willingness to learn from every experience. It means being receptive to new ideas and perspectives, seeking out opportunities for growth and development, and embracing challenges as opportunities for learning and self-improvement. By cultivating a learning mindset, individuals can maintain a sense of wonder and curiosity throughout life, and continuously expand their knowledge and skills.

Seeking out diverse learning experiences is another important aspect of lifelong learning. Exposure to a variety of perspectives, ideas, and disciplines stimulates creativity, critical thinking, and innovation. This may involve exploring subjects outside of one's comfort zone, engaging with people from different backgrounds and cultures, or pursuing interdisciplinary studies that integrate multiple fields of knowledge. By embracing diversity in learning, individuals can gain new insights, expand their worldview, and develop a deeper understanding of themselves and the world around them.

Setting learning goals and milestones is also essential for lifelong learning. Learning goals provide direction and motivation, and help individuals focus their learning efforts on areas that are important to them. Whether it's mastering a new skill, pursuing a passion project, or advancing in a career, setting clear and achievable learning goals helps individuals stay accountable and track their progress over time. Breaking larger goals down into smaller, manageable steps can make them more attainable and provide a sense of accomplishment along the way.

Creating a supportive learning environment is also important for lifelong learning. Surrounding oneself with people who support and encourage learning, whether it's friends, family members, mentors, or peers, can provide valuable feedback, guidance, and motivation. Participating in communities of practice, joining clubs or organizations, or attending networking events can also provide opportunities for collaboration, mentorship, and shared learning experiences. By building a supportive learning network, individuals can enhance their learning journey and achieve greater success and fulfillment.

Finally, reflecting on learning experiences is an important aspect of lifelong learning. Reflection involves taking time to review and evaluate what has been learned, identify strengths and areas for improvement, and consider how learning can be applied to future endeavors. Keeping a learning journal, engaging in self-assessment, or seeking feedback from others can help individuals deepen their understanding and integrate new knowledge and skills into their lives. By incorporating reflection into the learning process, individuals can enhance their learning outcomes and cultivate a deeper appreciation for the value of lifelong learning.

Chapter 22: Creative Expression

Creative expression is the process of communicating thoughts, emotions, and ideas through various forms of art, hobbies, and creative activities. It encompasses a wide range of artistic mediums, including visual arts, writing, music, dance, theater, crafting, and more. Engaging in creative expression allows individuals to explore their imagination, tap into their emotions, and express themselves in unique and meaningful ways. It provides a source of joy, fulfillment, and personal growth, and can serve as a form of self-care and stress relief.

The importance of creative expression lies in its ability to nourish the soul, stimulate the mind, and foster personal growth and well-being. Engaging in creative activities provides an outlet for self-expression and self-discovery, allowing individuals to explore their identity, values, and beliefs, and connect with others on a deeper level. Creative expression encourages experimentation, curiosity, and a willingness to take risks, which can lead to greater resilience, adaptability, and innovation in all areas of life.

One of the key principles of creative expression is embracing creativity as a process, rather than focusing solely on the end result. Creativity is not limited to artists or individuals with special talents; it's a natural and innate human ability that can be cultivated and developed through practice and exploration. By embracing creativity as a process of experimentation, play, and discovery, individuals can free themselves from self-judgment and perfectionism, and tap into their unique creative potential.

Another important aspect of creative expression is finding joy and fulfillment in the creative process itself, rather than solely seeking external validation or recognition. Engaging in creative activities provides a sense of flow, or "being in the zone," where time seems to stand still, and individuals are fully immersed in the present moment. This state of flow fosters a sense of joy, fulfillment, and well-being, and allows individuals to experience a deep sense of satisfaction and accomplishment from their creative endeavors.

Exploring different artistic mediums and creative outlets is also important for finding joy in art and hobbies. Creativity knows no bounds, and there are endless opportunities for artistic expression in various forms, from painting and drawing to writing, music, dance, and beyond. By exploring different mediums and creative outlets, individuals can discover new passions, talents, and interests, and expand their creative horizons. Whether it's experimenting with watercolors, learning to play a musical instrument, or trying out a new craft, the possibilities for creative expression are endless.

Creating a dedicated space for creativity and self-expression is another important aspect of finding joy in art and hobbies. Having a designated space where individuals can engage in creative activities free from distractions and interruptions can help foster a sense of focus, inspiration, and flow. This may be a corner of a room, a studio space, or simply a quiet spot where individuals can retreat to unleash their creativity and express themselves freely.

Fostering a mindset of curiosity and experimentation is also essential for finding joy in art and hobbies. Creativity thrives on curiosity and a willingness to explore new ideas, techniques, and possibilities. By approaching creative activities with an open mind and a sense of curiosity, individuals can discover new ways of seeing and experiencing the world, and unlock their creative potential in surprising and unexpected ways.

Engaging in creative expression as a form of self-care and stress relief is another important aspect of finding joy in art and hobbies. Creative activities provide a healthy outlet for processing emotions, reducing stress, and promoting relaxation and well-being. Whether it's journaling to express thoughts and feelings, painting to unwind after a long day, or playing music to lift the spirits, creative expression can be a powerful tool for self-care and personal growth.

Finally, sharing creative work with others and connecting with a community of fellow artists and creators can enhance the joy of art and hobbies. Sharing creative work allows individuals to receive feedback, encouragement, and support from others, and to experience a sense of connection and belonging through shared interests and experiences. Whether it's participating in art shows, joining a writing group, or sharing work online through social media or creative platforms, connecting with others can enrich the creative process and provide a sense of validation and affirmation.

Chapter 23: Decluttering Your Space

Decluttering your space is the process of simplifying and organizing your environment by removing unnecessary items, streamlining belongings, and creating a more functional and aesthetically pleasing living or working space. It involves assessing the items you own, decluttering them based on their usefulness and significance, and organizing them in a way that promotes clarity, efficiency, and peace of mind. Decluttering is not just about tidying up; it's about creating a space that supports your well-being, productivity, and overall quality of life.

The importance of decluttering your space lies in its ability to create a sense of calm, order, and harmony in your surroundings. Our physical environment has a profound impact on our mental and emotional well-being, and living or working in a cluttered and disorganized space can contribute to stress, anxiety, and feelings of overwhelm. Decluttering allows you to reclaim control over your environment, reduce visual and mental clutter, and create a space that feels spacious, inviting, and conducive to relaxation and focus.

One of the key principles of decluttering your space is adopting a minimalist mindset. Minimalism is a lifestyle philosophy that emphasizes simplicity, intentionality, and mindful consumption. It encourages individuals to focus on what truly matters to them, and to let go of excess possessions, distractions, and obligations that do not align with their values or goals. By embracing minimalism, you can create a space that is free from unnecessary clutter and distractions, and that allows you to focus on what brings you joy and fulfillment.

Another important aspect of decluttering your space is letting go of items that no longer serve a purpose or bring you joy. This involves assessing each item you own and determining whether it adds value to your life. Marie Kondo, author of "The Life-Changing Magic of Tidying Up," advocates for decluttering based on whether an item "sparks joy." If an item does not bring you joy or serve a practical purpose, it may be time to let it go. By decluttering your space in this way, you can create a more intentional and meaningful environment that reflects your values and priorities.

Creating functional storage solutions is also essential for decluttering your space. Effective storage solutions allow you to organize and store belongings in a way that maximizes space and accessibility. This may involve investing in storage containers, shelving units, or furniture with built-in storage options, as well as implementing organizational systems such as categorizing items by type or frequency of use. By creating functional storage solutions, you can keep your space tidy and organized, and make it easier to maintain a clutter-free environment in the long term.

Developing daily habits for maintaining a clutter-free environment is another important aspect of decluttering your space. Small, consistent actions such as tidying up at the end of each day, putting items back in their designated places after use, and regularly purging items you no longer need can help prevent clutter from accumulating over time. By incorporating these habits into your daily routine, you can keep your space organized and clutter-free with minimal effort.

Setting boundaries with belongings and resisting the urge to accumulate unnecessary items is also crucial for decluttering your space. In today's consumerist culture, it's easy to fall into the trap of buying more than we need or holding onto possessions out of a sense of obligation or attachment. By setting boundaries and being mindful of what you bring into your space, you can prevent clutter from accumulating and ensure that your environment remains simplified and streamlined.

Taking a mindful approach to decluttering your space involves being present and intentional throughout the process. This means taking the time to assess your belongings thoughtfully, considering their significance and impact on your life, and making conscious decisions about what to keep, donate, or discard. Mindful decluttering allows you to cultivate a greater awareness of your relationship with your possessions and create a space that supports your well-being and personal growth.

Chapter 24: Digital Detox

Digital detox refers to the intentional and temporary break from digital devices and technology to reduce stress, increase mindfulness, and reconnect with the physical world. It involves stepping away from screens such as smartphones, computers, tablets, and televisions, and limiting or abstaining from activities such as social media, email, gaming, and streaming services. Digital detoxes can vary in duration and intensity, ranging from a few hours to several days or weeks, and can be done individually or as part of a group or organized retreat. The goal of a digital detox is to restore balance in one's life, promote well-being, and foster a healthier relationship with technology.

The importance of digital detoxing lies in its ability to counteract the negative effects of excessive screen time and digital overload on mental, emotional, and physical well-being. In today's hyperconnected world, it's easy to become overwhelmed by the constant barrage of notifications, information, and stimuli from digital devices. Overuse of technology has been linked to increased stress, anxiety, depression, sleep disturbances, and decreased attention span and productivity. Digital detoxing provides an opportunity to step back, unplug, and recalibrate, allowing individuals to recharge their mental and emotional batteries, and reconnect with themselves and the world around them.

One of the key principles of digital detoxing is setting boundaries and establishing a healthy relationship with technology. This involves being mindful of how much time you spend on digital devices and the impact it has on your well-being, and taking proactive steps to limit screen time and create balance in your life. Setting boundaries may involve establishing designated tech-free zones or times, such as during meals, before bedtime, or on weekends, and sticking to them consistently. By setting boundaries, you can regain control over your digital habits and prioritize activities that nourish and enrich your life.

Another important aspect of digital detoxing is cultivating mindfulness and presence in everyday life. Mindfulness involves paying attention to the present moment with openness, curiosity, and acceptance, and being fully engaged in whatever you are doing, whether it's eating, walking, or spending time with loved ones. Digital devices often pull us out of the present moment and distract us from our immediate surroundings, making it difficult to fully experience and appreciate life as it unfolds. By disconnecting from screens and practicing mindfulness, you can cultivate a deeper sense of connection to yourself, others, and the world around you, and experience greater peace, clarity, and fulfillment.

Engaging in activities that promote well-being and self-care is another important aspect of digital detoxing. Instead of turning to screens for entertainment or distraction, consider activities that nourish your body, mind, and soul, such as spending time outdoors, exercising, reading, journaling, or practicing meditation or yoga. These activities not only provide a much-needed break from screens but also promote relaxation, stress reduction, and overall well-being. By prioritizing self-care and well-being, you can replenish your energy reserves and enhance your resilience in the face of digital overload.

Connecting with others in meaningful ways is also essential for digital detoxing. Digital devices have revolutionized the way we communicate and connect with others, but they can also undermine the quality of our relationships and social interactions. Excessive screen time can lead to feelings of loneliness, isolation, and disconnection from others, as face-to-face interactions are replaced by digital communication. Digital detoxing provides an opportunity to reconnect with loved ones in real life, whether it's through shared activities, meaningful conversations, or simply spending quality time together without the distraction of screens. By prioritizing real-life connections, you can strengthen your relationships, deepen your sense of belonging, and experience greater fulfillment and happiness.

Practicing gratitude and appreciation for the simple pleasures in life is another important aspect of digital detoxing. In today's fast-paced and hyperconnected world, it's easy to take the little things for granted and overlook the beauty and wonder of the world around us. Digital detoxing provides an opportunity to slow down, savor the moment, and cultivate gratitude for the simple joys of life, such as a beautiful sunset, a delicious meal, or a heartfelt conversation with a friend. By shifting your focus from screens to the present moment, you can develop a greater appreciation for life's blessings and find joy and fulfillment in the here and now.

Chapter 25: Mindful Consumption

Mindful consumption is the practice of making deliberate, conscious choices about what we buy, use, and consume in our daily lives. It involves being aware of the environmental, social, and ethical implications of our consumption habits, and making decisions that align with our values and priorities. Mindful consumption goes beyond simply buying less; it's about cultivating a deeper understanding of the impact our consumption has on ourselves, others, and the planet, and striving to make choices that promote sustainability, equity, and well-being.

The importance of mindful consumption lies in its potential to promote sustainability, reduce waste, and foster a more equitable and compassionate world. Our consumption habits have far-reaching implications for the environment, social justice, and human rights, and making mindful choices can help mitigate negative impacts and create positive change. By being mindful of what we buy, use, and consume, we can reduce our carbon footprint, conserve natural resources, support ethical and sustainable practices, and promote a more just and sustainable global economy.

One of the key principles of mindful consumption is understanding the true cost of the products and services we consume. This involves considering not only the financial cost but also the environmental and social costs associated with production, distribution, and disposal. Many products are produced under exploitative labor conditions, contribute to environmental degradation, or have negative impacts on communities and ecosystems. By considering the full lifecycle of products and services, from raw material extraction to end-of-life disposal, we can make more informed decisions and choose options that minimize harm and maximize benefits for people and the planet.

Another important aspect of mindful consumption is reducing waste and embracing a more minimalist lifestyle. Consumerism and overconsumption have led to a culture of excess and waste, with devastating consequences for the environment and future generations. Mindful consumption involves questioning our consumption habits and resisting the pressure to constantly acquire more stuff. By focusing on what truly brings value and meaning to our lives and letting go of the rest, we can reduce waste, simplify our lives, and live more sustainably.

Choosing products and services that align with our values and priorities is also essential for mindful consumption. This may involve supporting companies and brands that prioritize sustainability, ethical labor practices, and social responsibility, and avoiding those that engage in harmful or unethical practices. By voting with our dollars and supporting companies that share our values, we can drive positive change in the marketplace and encourage more responsible and sustainable business practices.

Practicing mindful consumption also involves being mindful of the resources we use and the impact they have on the environment. This includes conserving energy and water, reducing our carbon footprint, and minimizing our use of single-use plastics and other non-renewable resources. By being mindful of our consumption habits and making conscious choices to reduce our environmental impact, we can contribute to the health and sustainability of the planet for future generations.

Choosing quality over quantity is another important aspect of mindful consumption. In a culture that often prioritizes cheap and disposable goods, it can be tempting to prioritize quantity over quality. However, investing in high-quality, durable products that are built to last can actually be more sustainable in the long run, as they require less frequent replacement and reduce overall resource consumption. By choosing quality products that are made to last, we can reduce waste, save money in the long term, and minimize our environmental footprint.

Practicing gratitude and contentment is also essential for mindful consumption. In a society that constantly bombards us with messages of materialism and consumerism, it's easy to fall into the trap of always wanting more. Mindful consumption involves cultivating a sense of gratitude for what we already have and finding contentment in the present moment. By appreciating the abundance in our lives and recognizing that true happiness does not come from material possessions, we can reduce the impulse to consume and live more sustainably and authentically.

Chapter 26: Altruism and Volunteering

Altruism and volunteering embody the spirit of giving back to the community selflessly and without expectation of personal gain. It involves dedicating time, resources, and energy to support and uplift others, often with the aim of promoting the well-being of individuals, communities, or society as a whole. Altruism and volunteering take many forms, from volunteering at local nonprofits and charities to participating in community service projects, fundraising events, and acts of kindness towards others. The essence of altruism and volunteering lies in the desire to make a positive difference in the lives of others and contribute to the common good.

The importance of altruism and volunteering cannot be overstated. In a world faced with numerous challenges, from poverty and inequality to environmental degradation and social injustice, acts of kindness and generosity play a crucial role in building stronger, more resilient communities and creating positive change. Altruism and volunteering not only benefit those in need but also enrich the lives of the volunteers themselves, fostering a sense of connection, purpose, and fulfillment that comes from making a meaningful difference in the world.

One of the key principles of altruism and volunteering is compassion and empathy towards others. Compassion is the ability to recognize and empathize with the suffering of others and to take action to alleviate it. By cultivating compassion and empathy, individuals can develop a deeper understanding of the challenges faced by others and feel motivated to contribute to their well-being in whatever way they can. Whether it's volunteering at a homeless shelter, mentoring at-risk youth, or advocating for social justice causes, acts of altruism are rooted in a genuine concern for the welfare of others.

Another important aspect of altruism and volunteering is building a sense of community and belonging. Volunteering brings people together from diverse backgrounds and experiences, united by a common goal of making a positive impact in their community. Through shared experiences and collaborative efforts, volunteers develop meaningful connections and forge bonds that transcend individual differences. This sense of community and belonging not only strengthens social ties but also fosters a sense of solidarity and collective responsibility for the well-being of others.

Empowerment is also a key principle of altruism and volunteering. Empowerment involves recognizing and honoring the dignity, agency, and potential of every individual, and providing them with the support and resources they need to thrive. Volunteering programs that prioritize empowerment focus on building capacity, skills, and self-confidence in those they serve, rather than fostering dependency or perpetuating a sense of victimhood. By empowering individuals to take control of their lives and shape their own futures, volunteering efforts can create lasting positive change that extends far beyond the immediate impact of the service provided.

Creating positive social change is another important aspect of altruism and volunteering. Many of the most pressing challenges facing society today, from poverty and homelessness to environmental degradation and human rights violations, require collective action and systemic change to address effectively. Volunteering efforts that focus on advocacy, education, and community organizing can help raise awareness, mobilize support, and advocate for policy changes that address root causes and create more just and equitable societies. By working together to create positive social change, volunteers can have a transformative impact on their communities and the world.

Personal growth and development are also important benefits of altruism and volunteering. Engaging in acts of kindness and service can be a powerful catalyst for personal growth, helping individuals develop valuable skills, such as leadership, communication, and problem-solving, and gain a deeper understanding of themselves and others. Volunteering also provides opportunities for personal fulfillment and a sense of purpose, as individuals see the tangible impact of their efforts and feel a sense of pride and satisfaction in knowing that they are making a difference in the lives of others.

Chapter 27: Developing Patience

Developing patience is a multifaceted process that involves cultivating a mindset of acceptance, resilience, and inner peace while navigating life's inevitable delays, challenges, and uncertainties. It's about learning to wait gracefully, without becoming frustrated, anxious, or overwhelmed by circumstances beyond our control. Patience is not simply about waiting passively; it's about maintaining a sense of calm and equanimity in the face of adversity, and embracing the journey with openness, curiosity, and compassion.

The importance of developing patience cannot be overstated. In today's fast-paced and demanding world, patience is a valuable skill that enables us to navigate life's challenges with grace and resilience. Whether it's waiting in line, dealing with setbacks, or facing long-term goals and aspirations, patience allows us to persevere with a sense of calm and equanimity, rather than succumbing to frustration or impatience. Developing patience is essential for maintaining mental and emotional well-being, fostering healthy relationships, and achieving long-term success and fulfillment in all areas of life.

One of the key principles of developing patience is cultivating acceptance and surrender to the present moment. Acceptance involves acknowledging reality as it is, without judgment or resistance, and embracing the inherent uncertainty and unpredictability of life. By letting go of the need for control and surrendering to what is, we can cultivate a sense of peace and equanimity, even in the midst of challenging circumstances. Acceptance does not mean passivity or resignation; rather, it's about acknowledging our limitations and trusting in the natural unfolding of life.

Another important aspect of developing patience is reframing our perception of time and embracing the concept of divine timing. Divine timing is the belief that everything happens in its own perfect time, according to a higher plan or purpose beyond our understanding. By trusting in the inherent wisdom of the universe and surrendering to divine timing, we can release the pressure to rush or force outcomes, and instead cultivate patience and trust in the unfolding of life. This perspective shift allows us to let go of the need for immediate results and embrace the journey with faith and grace.

Practicing mindfulness and presence is also essential for developing patience. Mindfulness involves paying attention to the present moment with openness, curiosity, and acceptance, and cultivating a nonjudgmental awareness of our thoughts, feelings, and sensations. By practicing mindfulness, we can become more attuned to our inner experiences and better able to respond to life's challenges with clarity and equanimity. Mindfulness also helps us develop greater patience by enabling us to stay grounded and centered, even in the midst of difficult emotions or circumstances.

Building resilience and coping skills is another important aspect of developing patience. Resilience is the ability to bounce back from adversity and overcome obstacles with strength and grace. By cultivating resilience, we can develop the inner resources and coping strategies needed to navigate life's challenges with patience and perseverance. This may involve developing healthy coping mechanisms, such as meditation, exercise, or journaling, as well as seeking support from others when needed. By building resilience, we can weather life's storms with grace and emerge stronger and more resilient than ever before.

Practicing self-compassion and self-care is also essential for developing patience. Self-compassion involves treating ourselves with kindness, understanding, and acceptance, especially during times of difficulty or struggle. By practicing self-compassion, we can cultivate greater patience with ourselves and others, and develop a more compassionate and forgiving attitude towards our own imperfections and limitations. Self-care is also important for replenishing our energy reserves and maintaining mental and emotional well-being. By prioritizing self-care activities that nourish and rejuvenate us, we can build resilience and cultivate patience in the face of life's challenges.

Chapter 28: Overcoming Procrastination

Overcoming procrastination is a transformative journey that involves understanding the root causes of procrastination, cultivating self-awareness and self-discipline, and implementing effective strategies to break free from the cycle of delay and take action towards our goals and aspirations. Procrastination is a common challenge that many people face, characterized by the tendency to postpone or avoid tasks and responsibilities, often due to feelings of anxiety, fear, perfectionism, or overwhelm. Overcoming procrastination requires a combination of mindset shifts, behavioral changes, and practical techniques to increase motivation, focus, and productivity.

Understanding the root causes of procrastination is the first step towards overcoming it. Procrastination can stem from a variety of factors, including fear of failure or success, perfectionism, lack of clarity or direction, overwhelm, lack of motivation or interest, or simply habit. By identifying the underlying reasons for our procrastination tendencies, we can develop a deeper understanding of ourselves and our behavior, and begin to address the root causes that are holding us back from taking action.

One of the key principles of overcoming procrastination is cultivating self-awareness and mindfulness. Self-awareness involves observing our thoughts, feelings, and behaviors without judgment, and recognizing the patterns and triggers that contribute to procrastination. By becoming more mindful of our procrastination tendencies, we can develop greater insight into our motivations and habits, and begin to challenge and change unhelpful patterns of thinking and behavior.

Another important aspect of overcoming procrastination is cultivating self-discipline and willpower. Self-discipline is the ability to control our impulses, resist distractions, and stay focused on our goals and priorities, even in the face of temptation or discomfort. By strengthening our self-discipline muscles through regular practice and repetition, we can increase our ability to take action and overcome procrastination. This may involve setting clear goals, creating a structured routine, breaking tasks down into smaller, more manageable steps, and holding ourselves accountable for our actions.

Developing a growth mindset is also essential for overcoming procrastination. A growth mindset is the belief that our abilities and intelligence can be developed through effort, practice, and learning, rather than being fixed traits. By adopting a growth mindset, we can embrace challenges, learn from failures, and persist in the face of setbacks, rather than being derailed by fear of failure or perfectionism. Cultivating a growth mindset allows us to view procrastination as a temporary setback or learning opportunity, rather than a reflection of our abilities or worth.

Practicing self-compassion is another important aspect of overcoming procrastination. Self-compassion involves treating ourselves with kindness, understanding, and acceptance, especially during times of difficulty or struggle. Rather than beating ourselves up for procrastinating or falling short of our goals, we can practice self-compassion by acknowledging our efforts and progress, and offering ourselves the same kindness and encouragement that we would offer to a friend. By practicing self-compassion, we can reduce feelings of guilt or shame associated with procrastination, and develop a more positive and supportive inner dialogue.

Implementing practical strategies and techniques is also essential for overcoming procrastination and taking action now. These may include:

1. Breaking tasks down into smaller, more manageable steps.
2. Setting specific, achievable goals and deadlines.
3. Creating a structured routine and schedule.
4. Minimizing distractions and creating a conducive work

environment.

5. Using tools and techniques such as time-blocking, the Pomodoro Technique, or task prioritization.

6. Rewarding ourselves for taking action and achieving milestones.

7. Seeking support and accountability from friends, family, or a coach.

Chapter 29: Building a Support Network

Building a support network is a fundamental aspect of personal growth and well-being, involving the cultivation of relationships with individuals who provide encouragement, guidance, and emotional support. Your support network, often referred to as "your tribe," consists of people who uplift you, believe in you, and stand by you through life's ups and downs. These individuals may include family members, friends, mentors, colleagues, or members of communities or groups that share your interests, values, or goals. Building a strong support network is essential for navigating life's challenges, overcoming obstacles, and fostering resilience and personal growth.

The importance of building a support network cannot be overstated. Human beings are social creatures by nature, and we thrive on connection, belonging, and community. A strong support network provides us with a sense of belonging, validation, and acceptance, and serves as a source of comfort, encouragement, and strength during difficult times. Research has shown that having a strong support network is associated with better mental and physical health outcomes, including lower levels of stress, anxiety, and depression, and increased resilience and well-being.

One of the key principles of building a support network is cultivating reciprocity and mutual support. Relationships are a two-way street, and building a support network involves not only receiving support from others but also offering support in return. By cultivating a spirit of generosity, kindness, and empathy in our interactions with others, we can create a supportive and nurturing environment where everyone feels valued and cared for. This may involve listening actively, offering encouragement and validation, providing practical assistance when needed, or simply being present for someone in their time of need.

Another important aspect of building a support network is seeking out individuals who share your values, interests, or goals. Your support network should consist of people who understand and resonate with your unique perspective, and who support you in pursuing your dreams and aspirations. This may involve joining communities or groups that align with your interests or passions, such as hobby clubs, sports teams, volunteer organizations, or professional networks. By connecting with like-minded individuals who share your values and goals, you can build deeper, more meaningful relationships and create a sense of belonging and camaraderie.

Building a support network also involves being proactive and intentional in seeking out relationships and connections. While some relationships may naturally develop through shared experiences or mutual connections, others may require effort and initiative on your part. This may involve reaching out to acquaintances or colleagues to initiate conversations or activities, attending networking events or social gatherings, or joining online communities or support groups. By putting yourself out there and being open to new connections, you can expand your social circle and build a diverse and supportive network of relationships.

Practicing effective communication and boundaries is another important aspect of building a support network. Healthy relationships are built on a foundation of trust, respect, and clear communication, and it's important to communicate openly and honestly with others about your needs, boundaries, and expectations. This may involve setting boundaries around how much time and energy you can devote to supporting others, being assertive in expressing your needs and preferences, and being receptive to feedback and constructive criticism from others. By practicing effective communication and boundaries, you can cultivate deeper, more authentic relationships and create a supportive and respectful environment for everyone involved.

Nurturing and maintaining your support network require ongoing effort and investment. This may involve reaching out to friends or family members regularly to check in and catch up, scheduling regular social activities or gatherings, or participating in group activities or events. It's also important to be proactive in offering support and assistance to others when they need it, and to be willing to ask for help when you need it yourself. By nurturing your support network and investing time and energy into your relationships, you can create a strong, resilient, and supportive community that will be there for you through life's ups and downs.

Chapter 30: Habit Stacking

Habit stacking is a powerful strategy for behavior change that involves linking new habits to existing routines or behaviors to create a sequence of actions that reinforce each other and lead to desired outcomes. It's based on the idea that small changes, when consistently applied and integrated into our daily routines, can lead to significant and lasting results over time. Habit stacking leverages the power of consistency, repetition, and association to make behavior change easier and more sustainable, allowing individuals to build new habits gradually and incrementally.

The importance of habit stacking lies in its ability to simplify behavior change and make it more manageable and sustainable. Many people struggle to adopt new habits or stick to resolutions because they try to make too many changes at once or rely on willpower alone to sustain their efforts. Habit stacking offers a more systematic and structured approach to behavior change, allowing individuals to build new habits incrementally and integrate them into their existing routines and lifestyles. By linking new habits to existing cues or behaviors, habit stacking creates a sequence of actions that become automatic and effortless over time, making behavior change easier and more sustainable in the long run.

One of the key principles of habit stacking is starting small and focusing on incremental progress. Instead of trying to overhaul your entire lifestyle overnight, begin by identifying one or two small habits that you want to develop or improve, and focus on integrating them into your daily routines. This could be as simple as drinking a glass of water before breakfast, taking a five-minute walk after lunch, or practicing gratitude before bed. By starting small and building momentum gradually, you can increase your chances of success and avoid feeling overwhelmed or discouraged by trying to make too many changes at once.

Another important aspect of habit stacking is linking new habits to existing cues or behaviors. This involves identifying existing routines or activities in your daily life that can serve as triggers or reminders for your new habits. For example, if you want to start a meditation practice, you could link it to your morning routine by meditating for five minutes immediately after brushing your teeth. By associating your new habit with an existing cue or behavior, you can leverage the power of association to make the new habit more automatic and ingrained over time.

Creating a habit stack involves identifying a sequence of actions that flow naturally from one another and reinforce each other's effects. This could be a series of small habits that you perform in a specific order, such as stretching, journaling, and reading before bed, or a set of actions that you perform in response to a particular cue or trigger, such as drinking a glass of water, taking a deep breath, and practicing mindfulness when you feel stressed or anxious. By creating a habit stack, you can streamline your routines and make behavior change more efficient and effective.

Consistency is key when it comes to habit stacking. To reap the benefits of habit stacking, it's important to practice your new habits consistently and integrate them into your daily routines until they become automatic and ingrained. This may require patience and persistence, as building new habits takes time and effort. However, by focusing on small, manageable changes and staying committed to your goals, you can gradually build momentum and make lasting changes to your behavior and lifestyle.

The benefits of habit stacking are numerous and far-reaching. By combining small changes into a sequence of actions, habit stacking allows you to leverage the power of consistency, repetition, and association to make behavior change easier and more sustainable. Habit stacking can help you develop new habits, break old habits, and create positive routines that support your goals and aspirations. It can also increase your efficiency and productivity by streamlining your routines and eliminating decision fatigue. Additionally, habit stacking can improve your overall well-being by helping you develop healthy habits and routines that contribute to your physical, mental, and emotional health.

Chapter 31: Embracing Change

Embracing change is a transformative process that involves cultivating resilience, flexibility, and openness to new possibilities as we navigate the inevitable transitions and challenges that life brings. Change is a constant and natural part of life, and our ability to adapt and thrive in the face of change is essential for personal growth, fulfillment, and well-being. Embracing change requires us to let go of old patterns, beliefs, and attachments that no longer serve us, and to embrace uncertainty, discomfort, and the unknown with courage, curiosity, and optimism.

The importance of embracing change cannot be overstated. In today's rapidly changing and unpredictable world, our ability to adapt and thrive in the face of change is essential for personal and professional success, resilience, and well-being. Whether it's changes in our relationships, careers, health, or environment, learning to embrace change allows us to navigate life's transitions with greater ease, confidence, and resilience. Embracing change also opens us up to new opportunities, experiences, and possibilities for growth and self-discovery, enriching our lives in ways we may never have imagined.

One of the key principles of embracing change is cultivating resilience and adaptability. Resilience is the ability to bounce back from adversity and overcome challenges with strength and grace. By cultivating resilience, we can develop the inner resources and coping skills needed to navigate life's transitions with courage and resilience. This may involve developing a growth mindset, practicing self-compassion, seeking support from others, and finding meaning and purpose in difficult circumstances. Adaptability is the ability to adjust to new circumstances and environments and to thrive in the face of change. By cultivating adaptability, we can learn to embrace uncertainty, take risks, and explore new opportunities with confidence and optimism.

Another important aspect of embracing change is letting go of resistance and surrendering to the natural flow of life. Resistance to change often stems from fear, uncertainty, or attachment to the familiar, and can prevent us from fully embracing new opportunities and experiences. By letting go of resistance and surrendering to the natural flow of life, we can open ourselves up to new possibilities, growth, and transformation. This may involve practicing mindfulness and acceptance, reframing our perception of change as an opportunity for growth and learning, and releasing attachments to outcomes or expectations.

Cultivating self-awareness and self-reflection is also essential for embracing change. Change often triggers a range of emotions, including fear, anxiety, sadness, and excitement, and it's important to acknowledge and process these emotions in a healthy and constructive way. By cultivating self-awareness and self-reflection, we can develop a deeper understanding of our reactions to change and uncover underlying beliefs, patterns, and motivations that may be holding us back. This may involve journaling, meditation, therapy, or other practices that promote self-awareness and introspection.

Practicing flexibility and adaptability is another key aspect of embracing change. Flexibility involves being open to new ideas, perspectives, and possibilities, and willing to adjust our plans and expectations in response to changing circumstances. By practicing flexibility, we can adapt more easily to unexpected changes and setbacks, and approach new challenges with a sense of curiosity, creativity, and resilience. This may involve reframing setbacks as opportunities for growth and learning, seeking feedback and input from others, and being willing to experiment and take risks in pursuit of our goals and aspirations.

Finding support and connection is also essential for embracing change. Change can be challenging and overwhelming at times, and having a strong support network of friends, family, mentors, and peers can provide encouragement, guidance, and perspective during times of transition. By reaching out to others for support and connection, we can feel less alone and more empowered to navigate life's changes with confidence and resilience. This may involve joining support groups, seeking out mentors or coaches, or simply reaching out to friends and loved ones for a listening ear and a shoulder to lean on.

Chapter 32: Mindful Breathing

Mindful breathing is a transformative practice that involves bringing conscious awareness to the breath, using it as a focal point to anchor our attention in the present moment. It's a fundamental aspect of mindfulness meditation and has been practiced for centuries in various contemplative traditions around the world. Mindful breathing involves paying attention to the sensations of the breath as it enters and leaves the body, observing its rhythm and flow without judgment or attachment. By harnessing the power of breath, mindful breathing can help reduce stress, promote relaxation, improve concentration, and cultivate greater self-awareness and emotional resilience.

The importance of mindful breathing lies in its ability to connect us with the present moment and promote a sense of calm, clarity, and centeredness. In today's fast-paced and stressful world, many of us are constantly on the go, juggling multiple responsibilities and distractions, and our minds are often preoccupied with worries, regrets, or anxieties about the past or future. Mindful breathing offers a simple yet powerful antidote to this habitual pattern of mind-wandering, allowing us to anchor our attention in the present moment and find refuge in the here and now.

One of the key principles of mindful breathing is cultivating awareness and nonjudgmental acceptance of our experience. This involves observing the sensations of the breath with curiosity, openness, and kindness, and allowing them to unfold naturally without trying to change or manipulate them in any way. By cultivating a nonjudgmental attitude towards our experience, we can develop greater self-awareness and emotional resilience, and learn to respond to our thoughts, feelings, and sensations with greater clarity and equanimity.

Another important aspect of mindful breathing is cultivating concentration and focus. The breath serves as a focal point for our attention, allowing us to anchor our awareness in the present moment and quiet the restless chatter of the mind. By focusing our attention on the sensations of the breath, we can train our minds to become more alert, attentive, and focused, and develop greater clarity and insight into our inner experience. This can have profound benefits for our mental and emotional well-being, helping us reduce stress, anxiety, and rumination, and improve our ability to concentrate and make wise choices in our lives.

Promoting relaxation and stress reduction is also a key benefit of mindful breathing. The breath is intimately connected to our nervous system, and by regulating our breath, we can influence our physiological state and promote a sense of relaxation and calm. Mindful breathing activates the parasympathetic nervous system, which is responsible for the body's "rest and digest" response, helping to counteract the stress response and promote relaxation and well-being. By practicing mindful breathing regularly, we can reduce the harmful effects of chronic stress and cultivate a greater sense of ease, balance, and resilience in our lives.

Practicing mindful breathing is relatively simple and can be done anywhere, at any time, without the need for special equipment or training. To begin, find a comfortable seated or lying position and close your eyes if that feels comfortable for you. Take a few deep breaths to center yourself and relax your body, then bring your attention to the sensations of the breath as it enters and leaves your body. Notice the rise and fall of your chest or abdomen, the sensation of air flowing in and out of your nostrils, and any other sensations that arise as you breathe. If your mind wanders, gently bring your attention back to the breath without judgment or self-criticism, and continue to observe the sensations of the breath with openness and curiosity.

Incorporating mindful breathing into your daily routine can have profound benefits for your mental, emotional, and physical well-being. You can practice mindful breathing for just a few minutes each day or integrate it into other activities, such as during moments of stress or overwhelm, before bed to promote relaxation and sleep, or during daily tasks such as walking or eating to bring greater presence and awareness to your experience. By harnessing the power of breath through mindful breathing, you can cultivate greater calm, clarity, and resilience in your life, and find greater peace and fulfillment in the present moment.

Chapter 33: Visualization Techniques

Visualization techniques are powerful tools for harnessing the creative power of the mind to imagine and manifest our desires, goals, and aspirations. Visualization involves using mental imagery to vividly imagine specific outcomes or scenarios, engaging our senses, emotions, and imagination to create a compelling and realistic experience in our minds. By visualizing our success and desired outcomes in detail, we can activate the subconscious mind, align our thoughts and beliefs with our goals, and increase our motivation, confidence, and belief in our ability to achieve our dreams.

The importance of visualization techniques lies in their ability to harness the power of the mind to create our reality. Our thoughts and beliefs have a profound influence on our behavior, actions, and outcomes, and visualization techniques provide a powerful tool for harnessing the creative power of the mind to shape our reality in alignment with our goals and aspirations. By vividly imagining our success and desired outcomes, we can program our subconscious mind with positive beliefs and expectations, and create a mental blueprint for achieving our dreams.

One of the key principles of visualization techniques is creating a clear and detailed mental image of your desired outcome. The more vivid and detailed your visualization, the more effectively it will engage your subconscious mind and align your thoughts, beliefs, and actions with your goals. When visualizing your success, use all of your senses to create a rich and immersive experience in your mind, imagining what you will see, hear, feel, smell, and taste as you achieve your goals. Visualize yourself succeeding in specific situations or scenarios, and immerse yourself in the emotions and sensations of accomplishment, joy, and fulfillment that accompany your success.

Another important aspect of visualization techniques is cultivating a sense of belief and confidence in your ability to achieve your goals.

Visualization is not just about creating mental images; it's also about cultivating the thoughts, beliefs, and emotions that support your success. As you visualize your success, cultivate a sense of confidence, self-assurance, and belief in your ability to achieve your goals. Affirm positive statements and beliefs about yourself and your capabilities, and focus on the strengths, skills, and qualities that will help you succeed. By aligning your thoughts and beliefs with your goals, you can increase your motivation, confidence, and resilience in the face of challenges and setbacks.

Practicing consistency and repetition is also essential for effective visualization. Like any skill or habit, visualization requires regular practice and reinforcement to become more ingrained and effective over time. Set aside dedicated time each day to practice visualization, ideally in a quiet and relaxed environment where you won't be interrupted. Consistency is key, so make visualization a regular part of your daily routine, and practice it with focused attention and intention. The more consistently you practice visualization, the more effectively you will be able to harness its power to create positive changes in your life.

Using visualization techniques in conjunction with other strategies and techniques can enhance their effectiveness and amplify their impact. For example, you can combine visualization with affirmations, goal-setting, action planning, and other techniques to create a comprehensive approach to goal achievement and personal development. Set specific, measurable, and achievable goals, and use visualization to imagine yourself achieving them in vivid detail. Create action plans and take concrete steps towards your goals, and use visualization to reinforce your commitment, motivation, and belief in your ability to succeed. By integrating visualization techniques into a holistic approach to goal achievement, you can maximize your chances of success and create lasting positive change in your life.

Chapter 34: Journaling for Growth

Journaling for growth is a transformative practice that involves reflecting on our thoughts, feelings, experiences, and goals through the written word. It's a versatile and powerful tool for self-discovery, self-expression, and personal development, allowing us to explore our innermost thoughts and emotions, gain insights into ourselves and our lives, and track our progress and growth over time. Journaling for growth encompasses a wide range of techniques and approaches, from free writing and stream-of-consciousness journaling to structured prompts and exercises designed to stimulate reflection and introspection.

The importance of journaling for growth lies in its ability to provide a safe and supportive space for self-reflection and exploration. In today's fast-paced and demanding world, many of us are constantly on the go, juggling multiple responsibilities and distractions, and our minds are often preoccupied with worries, regrets, or anxieties about the past or future. Journaling offers a way to slow down, pause, and reconnect with ourselves, allowing us to process our thoughts and emotions, gain clarity and perspective, and deepen our understanding of ourselves and our lives.

One of the key principles of journaling for growth is creating a safe and nonjudgmental space for self-expression. Journaling is not about writing perfectly crafted prose or adhering to rigid rules or conventions; it's about allowing yourself to express yourself freely and authentically, without fear of judgment or criticism. Give yourself permission to write honestly and openly about whatever is on your mind, whether it's your hopes and dreams, your fears and insecurities, or your everyday experiences and observations. Remember that there are no right or wrong answers in journaling, and that the goal is simply to explore and reflect on your inner world with curiosity, compassion, and self-acceptance.

Another important aspect of journaling for growth is cultivating self-awareness and introspection. Journaling provides an opportunity to tune into our inner thoughts, feelings, and intuition, and to develop a deeper understanding of ourselves and our lives. By regularly reflecting on our experiences and exploring our thoughts and emotions through writing, we can gain insights into our patterns, beliefs, and motivations, and identify areas for growth and development. This increased self-awareness can empower us to make more conscious choices, cultivate healthier habits and relationships, and live more authentically and intentionally.

Practicing consistency and regularity is also essential for effective journaling for growth. Like any skill or habit, journaling requires regular practice and commitment to become more ingrained and effective over time. Set aside dedicated time each day or week to journal, ideally in a quiet and comfortable environment where you won't be interrupted. Consistency is key, so make journaling a regular part of your routine, and commit to showing up for yourself and your growth journey. The more consistently you journal, the more you will be able to reap the benefits of self-reflection and introspection, and the more you will be able to track your progress and growth over time.

Using prompts and exercises can enhance the effectiveness of journaling for growth and stimulate deeper reflection and insight. Prompts are open-ended questions or statements designed to inspire reflection and introspection, while exercises are structured activities or techniques designed to facilitate self-discovery and personal development. There are countless journaling prompts and exercises available online and in books, covering a wide range of topics and themes, from gratitude and self-compassion to goal-setting and values clarification. Experiment with different prompts and exercises to find what resonates with you, and don't be afraid to get creative and adapt them to suit your unique needs and preferences.

Chapter 35: The Role of Humor

Humor plays a multifaceted role in our lives, serving as a source of joy, relief, connection, and resilience in the face of life's challenges and adversities. It encompasses a wide range of expressions, from laughter and wit to satire and irony, and has been celebrated throughout history and across cultures for its ability to uplift spirits, foster social bonds, and bring a sense of lightness and perspective to even the darkest of circumstances. The role of humor extends far beyond mere entertainment; it permeates every aspect of our lives, influencing our relationships, our health, our creativity, and our ability to navigate the complexities of the human experience with grace and resilience.

One of the key roles of humor is its ability to bring joy and laughter into our lives, even in the midst of difficult times. Laughter is a universal language that transcends cultural, linguistic, and social barriers, and has the power to unite people from all walks of life in moments of shared hilarity and mirth. Whether it's a belly laugh with friends, a playful joke with coworkers, or a funny meme shared on social media, humor has the ability to brighten our day, lighten our mood, and remind us not to take life too seriously.

Humor also serves as a powerful coping mechanism for dealing with stress, adversity, and uncertainty. In times of crisis or hardship, humor can provide a much-needed release valve for pent-up tension and anxiety, allowing us to momentarily escape from our worries and find relief in laughter. By reframing difficult situations in a humorous light, we can gain a sense of perspective and resilience, and find the strength to face our challenges with courage and grace. Humor helps us to maintain a sense of optimism and hope in the face of adversity, reminding us that even in the darkest of times, there is always something to laugh about.

Moreover, humor plays a crucial role in fostering social bonds and strengthening relationships. Shared laughter creates a sense of camaraderie and connection among individuals, breaking down barriers and building bridges between people from different backgrounds and perspectives. Humor serves as a powerful social lubricant, smoothing over awkwardness and tension in social interactions, and creating a sense of warmth and intimacy between friends, family members, and colleagues. By sharing jokes, anecdotes, and humorous stories, we deepen our connections with others and create lasting memories that strengthen our relationships and enrich our lives.

In addition to its social and emotional benefits, humor has been shown to have numerous health benefits as well. Laughter has been linked to a wide range of physiological and psychological benefits, including reduced stress, improved immune function, increased pain tolerance, and enhanced mood. Laughter triggers the release of endorphins, the body's natural feel-good chemicals, which promote a sense of well-being and relaxation. Regular laughter has also been associated with lower levels of stress hormones, such as cortisol and adrenaline, and a reduced risk of chronic diseases, such as heart disease and depression. By incorporating humor into our daily lives, we can promote our physical and mental health and enhance our overall quality of life.

Furthermore, humor plays a vital role in fostering creativity, innovation, and problem-solving. A playful and lighthearted approach to life encourages us to think outside the box, explore new ideas, and take risks in pursuit of our goals. By embracing humor and embracing failure, we create a culture of experimentation and innovation, where mistakes are seen as opportunities for growth and learning rather than sources of shame or embarrassment. Humor stimulates our imagination and creativity, helping us to approach challenges with curiosity, flexibility, and resilience, and to find novel solutions to complex problems.

Chapter 36: Spiritual Practices

Spiritual practices encompass a diverse array of rituals, traditions, and disciplines aimed at cultivating a deeper connection with something greater than ourselves, whether it be the divine, the universe, nature, or the collective consciousness of humanity. These practices are deeply rooted in ancient wisdom and have been passed down through generations, shaping cultures, religions, and belief systems around the world. While the specific forms and expressions of spiritual practices vary widely across different traditions and cultures, they all share a common goal: to nurture the human spirit, foster a sense of meaning and purpose, and awaken a deeper sense of connection and belonging in the world.

The importance of spiritual practices lies in their ability to nourish the soul and cultivate a deeper sense of connection and purpose in our lives. In today's fast-paced and materialistic world, many of us find ourselves disconnected from our inner selves, the natural world, and the deeper mysteries of existence. Spiritual practices offer a pathway back to wholeness and harmony, providing us with tools and techniques for exploring the deeper dimensions of our being and awakening to the sacredness of life. Whether through prayer, meditation, ritual, or sacred ceremony, spiritual practices invite us to slow down, quiet the mind, and attune to the deeper currents of wisdom and guidance that flow through us and around us.

One of the key principles of spiritual practices is cultivating presence and mindfulness. Presence involves being fully awake and attentive to the present moment, without judgment or attachment to the past or future. Spiritual practices such as meditation, mindfulness, and contemplative prayer provide us with opportunities to cultivate presence and mindfulness, allowing us to anchor our awareness in the here and now, and to experience the richness and beauty of life as it unfolds moment by moment. By cultivating presence and mindfulness, we can deepen our connection with something greater than ourselves and open ourselves to the wisdom and guidance that resides within us and all around us.

Another important aspect of spiritual practices is cultivating reverence and awe for the mysteries of existence. Spiritual practices invite us to contemplate the vastness of the cosmos, the beauty of nature, and the miracle of life itself, and to recognize the divine presence that animates all creation. Whether through sacred rituals, ceremonies, or moments of quiet contemplation, spiritual practices help us to cultivate a sense of reverence and awe for the wonders of existence, and to recognize our place within the larger web of life. By cultivating reverence and awe, we can awaken to the sacredness of life and deepen our appreciation for the interconnectedness of all things.

Spiritual practices also serve as a powerful means of self-discovery and personal transformation. Through practices such as meditation, prayer, journaling, and ritual, we can explore the depths of our own inner landscape, confront our fears and limitations, and tap into our inner wisdom and intuition. Spiritual practices provide us with tools and techniques for navigating the complexities of the human experience, and for cultivating qualities such as compassion, forgiveness, gratitude, and resilience. By engaging in spiritual practices, we can embark on a journey of self-discovery and personal growth, and uncover the hidden dimensions of our being.

Moreover, spiritual practices offer a pathway to connection and community. Whether through shared rituals, ceremonies, or gatherings, spiritual practices provide opportunities for individuals to come together in a spirit of love, unity, and mutual support. Spiritual communities offer a sense of belonging and belongingness, and provide spaces where individuals can find solace, inspiration, and guidance on their spiritual journey. By participating in spiritual communities, individuals can deepen their connection with something greater than themselves, and experience the transformative power of collective prayer, meditation, and celebration.

Chapter 37: Finding Balance

Finding balance in life is a perpetual pursuit, an ongoing process of juggling the various demands and responsibilities that come our way while striving to maintain a sense of equilibrium, harmony, and well-being. It encompasses the delicate art of managing our time, energy, and resources in a way that honors our priorities, values, and goals, while also attending to the diverse facets of our lives, including work, family, relationships, health, and personal interests. While achieving balance may seem like an elusive goal in today's fast-paced and demanding world, it's an essential aspect of living a fulfilling and meaningful life, allowing us to cultivate a sense of wholeness, resilience, and fulfillment in all areas of our lives.

The importance of finding balance lies in its ability to promote overall well-being and enhance the quality of our lives. In today's hyper-connected and hyper-competitive world, many of us find ourselves caught in a perpetual cycle of busyness and stress, constantly striving to meet the demands and expectations of work, family, and society. However, when we neglect our own needs and priorities in favor of external obligations and pressures, we risk burnout, exhaustion, and disconnection from ourselves and those we love. Finding balance allows us to step back from the relentless pace of modern life, reevaluate our priorities, and make intentional choices that honor our well-being and fulfillment.

One of the key principles of finding balance is prioritizing self-care and well-being. Self-care encompasses a wide range of practices and activities aimed at nurturing our physical, emotional, and mental health, and replenishing our energy and vitality. This may include getting enough sleep, eating nourishing foods, exercising regularly, practicing mindfulness and relaxation techniques, and engaging in activities that bring us joy and fulfillment. By prioritizing self-care, we can replenish our energy reserves, reduce stress and burnout, and cultivate a greater sense of resilience and well-being in our lives.

Another important aspect of finding balance is setting boundaries and managing our time effectively. Boundaries are essential for protecting our time, energy, and resources, and for ensuring that we allocate them in alignment with our priorities and values. This may involve learning to say no to requests and obligations that don't align with our priorities, delegating tasks and responsibilities when appropriate, and carving out time for rest, relaxation, and recreation. By setting boundaries and managing our time effectively, we can create space for the things that matter most to us, and avoid overextending ourselves or spreading ourselves too thin.

Finding balance also requires cultivating a sense of presence and mindfulness in our daily lives. Presence involves being fully engaged and attentive to the present moment, without being consumed by worries or regrets about the past, or anxieties about the future. Mindfulness practices such as meditation, yoga, and deep breathing can help us cultivate presence and awareness, and create a sense of spaciousness and clarity in our minds. By bringing mindful awareness to our daily activities and interactions, we can cultivate a greater sense of balance, peace, and fulfillment in our lives.

Moreover, finding balance involves nurturing our relationships and connections with others. Relationships are a fundamental aspect of human life, providing us with love, support, and companionship, and enriching our lives in countless ways. However, maintaining healthy relationships requires time, effort, and attention, and can sometimes be challenging to balance with other demands and responsibilities. Finding balance in our relationships involves prioritizing quality time with loved ones, nurturing open and honest communication, and cultivating a sense of connection and intimacy. By investing in our relationships and connections with others, we can deepen our sense of belonging and fulfillment, and create a support network that sustains us through life's ups and downs.

Chapter 38: Celebrating Small Wins

Celebrating small wins is a powerful practice that involves acknowledging and appreciating the incremental achievements and milestones that we make on our journey towards our goals. It's about recognizing the progress we've made, no matter how small or seemingly insignificant, and taking the time to celebrate and savor these moments of success. While it's natural to focus on the big goals and milestones in life, celebrating small wins reminds us that progress is made step by step, and that each small victory brings us closer to our ultimate objectives.

The importance of celebrating small wins lies in its ability to boost motivation, confidence, and morale, and to foster a positive and resilient mindset. In today's fast-paced and achievement-oriented culture, it's easy to become fixated on the big goals and milestones, and to overlook the small victories and achievements that occur along the way. However, research has shown that celebrating small wins can have a profound impact on our motivation and well-being, helping us to stay focused, energized, and engaged in our pursuits. By acknowledging and celebrating our progress, we reinforce our sense of competence and efficacy, and cultivate a greater sense of optimism and resilience in the face of challenges and setbacks.

One of the key principles of celebrating small wins is cultivating a growth mindset. A growth mindset is the belief that our abilities and intelligence can be developed through effort, perseverance, and learning. When we adopt a growth mindset, we see challenges and setbacks as opportunities for growth and learning, rather than as indicators of our limitations or shortcomings. Celebrating small wins reinforces a growth mindset by highlighting our progress and accomplishments, and reminding us of the progress we've made, no matter how small or incremental. By cultivating a growth mindset and celebrating small wins, we can foster a sense of optimism and resilience, and approach our goals with greater confidence and determination.

Another important aspect of celebrating small wins is cultivating gratitude and appreciation for the journey. Gratitude is the practice of recognizing and appreciating the good things in our lives, and celebrating small wins is a powerful way to cultivate gratitude and appreciation for the progress we've made. When we take the time to acknowledge and celebrate our small victories, we cultivate a sense of gratitude for the opportunities and resources that have supported our progress, and for the effort and perseverance that we've invested in our pursuits. By cultivating gratitude and appreciation, we can cultivate a sense of fulfillment and contentment in our lives, and approach our goals with a greater sense of joy and enthusiasm.

Moreover, celebrating small wins helps to build momentum and sustain progress over time. When we acknowledge and celebrate our progress, no matter how small or incremental, we reinforce our sense of accomplishment and motivation, and create positive feedback loops that fuel further progress and success. By celebrating small wins regularly, we create a sense of momentum and progress that propels us forward towards our goals, and helps us to overcome obstacles and setbacks along the way. By building momentum and sustaining progress over time, we increase our chances of achieving our goals and realizing our dreams.

Chapter 39: Sustaining Motivation

Sustaining motivation is a dynamic process that involves maintaining the drive, energy, and enthusiasm needed to pursue our goals and aspirations over the long term. While initial bursts of motivation can propel us forward and inspire action, sustaining motivation requires ongoing effort, commitment, and resilience in the face of challenges, setbacks, and distractions. It's about cultivating a mindset and adopting strategies that help us stay focused, engaged, and inspired, even when the journey becomes challenging or demanding.

The importance of sustaining motivation lies in its role as a driving force behind our actions and achievements. Motivation is what fuels our ambition, guides our behavior, and propels us towards our goals and aspirations. Without sustained motivation, it's easy to become discouraged or disheartened when faced with obstacles or setbacks, and to lose sight of the vision and purpose that inspired us to pursue our goals in the first place. By cultivating the ability to sustain motivation, we can stay focused, resilient, and committed to our goals, even in the face of adversity, and continue making progress towards our dreams.

One of the key principles of sustaining motivation is cultivating a clear sense of purpose and direction. Purpose is the underlying reason or motivation behind our goals and aspirations, and having a clear sense of purpose can provide us with a powerful source of inspiration and drive. When we know why we're pursuing a particular goal or aspiration, and how it aligns with our values, passions, and aspirations, we're more likely to stay motivated and committed, even when the journey becomes challenging or demanding. By cultivating a clear sense of purpose and direction, we can stay focused on our goals, overcome obstacles, and sustain motivation over the long term.

Another important aspect of sustaining motivation is setting realistic and achievable goals. Goals that are specific, measurable, attainable, relevant, and time-bound (SMART) provide us with clear targets to aim for and help us stay focused and motivated. When we set goals that are too vague or unrealistic, it's easy to become overwhelmed or discouraged when progress is slow or setbacks occur. By setting realistic and achievable goals, we can break our larger aspirations into smaller, manageable steps, and celebrate our progress along the way. This helps us maintain a sense of momentum and progress, and keeps us motivated to continue moving forward towards our objectives.

Moreover, sustaining motivation involves cultivating a growth mindset and embracing failure as an opportunity for learning and growth. A growth mindset is the belief that our abilities and intelligence can be developed through effort, perseverance, and learning. When we adopt a growth mindset, we see challenges and setbacks as opportunities for growth and learning, rather than as indicators of our limitations or shortcomings. By embracing failure as a natural part of the learning process, we can cultivate resilience, perseverance, and a willingness to take risks in pursuit of our goals. This helps us stay motivated and engaged, even when the journey becomes difficult or uncertain.

Additionally, sustaining motivation involves taking care of our physical, emotional, and mental well-being. Our overall well-being has a profound impact on our motivation, energy levels, and ability to stay focused and engaged. When we neglect our physical health, for example, by not getting enough sleep, exercise, or nutritious food, it's easy to feel tired, lethargic, and unmotivated. Similarly, when we neglect our emotional and mental well-being, by not managing stress, practicing self-care, or seeking support when needed, it's easy to feel overwhelmed, anxious, or burnt out. By prioritizing self-care and well-being, we can replenish our energy reserves, reduce stress, and cultivate a greater sense of resilience, vitality, and motivation in our lives.

Chapter 40: Conclusion

In the grand tapestry of life, embarking on a journey toward lasting change is both a profound quest and a deeply personal odyssey. As we navigate the labyrinth of our aspirations, challenges, triumphs, and setbacks, we embark on a transformational journey that shapes not only our external circumstances but also our inner landscape. Throughout this expedition, we encounter countless crossroads, each offering opportunities for growth, self-discovery, and renewal. And as we traverse these pathways, we are guided by the guiding light of our intentions, the compass of our values, and the resilience of our spirit.

Your journey to lasting change begins with a single step—a moment of inspiration, a flicker of curiosity, or a spark of determination that ignites the flame of possibility within you. It's a journey of self-discovery and self-mastery, of uncovering hidden truths, unlocking dormant potentials, and unleashing the power of your authenticity. It's a journey of courage and commitment, of confronting your fears, embracing your vulnerabilities, and daring to dream boldly in the face of uncertainty.

Along the way, you'll encounter challenges and obstacles that test your resolve and resilience. You'll face moments of doubt, discouragement, and despair, where the path ahead seems shrouded in darkness, and the weight of your burdens threatens to overwhelm you. But it's in these moments of adversity that your true strength and character are revealed. It's in these moments that you discover the depths of your courage, the resilience of your spirit, and the unwavering faith that carries you through the storm.

As you journey toward lasting change, remember that transformation is not a destination but a process—a continuous evolution of growth, learning, and becoming. It's about embracing the journey itself—the highs and lows, the twists and turns, the moments of joy and sorrow—as an integral part of your transformation. It's about surrendering to the flow of life, trusting in the wisdom of your intuition, and embracing the unknown with an open heart and mind.

Throughout your journey, cultivate a spirit of curiosity, openness, and humility. Be willing to explore new horizons, challenge old beliefs, and embrace new perspectives. Be open to feedback, guidance, and support from others who walk alongside you on your journey. And above all, be gentle and compassionate with yourself, recognizing that change takes time, patience, and perseverance, and that every step forward is a victory worth celebrating.

As you reflect on your journey to lasting change, remember that you are the author of your own story—the architect of your destiny, and the master of your fate. You have within you the power to create the life you desire, to manifest your deepest dreams, and to realize your fullest potential. Trust in your inner wisdom, follow the whispers of your heart, and embrace the journey with courage, grace, and gratitude.

Your journey to lasting change is a sacred pilgrimage—a sacred journey of self-discovery, growth, and transformation. It's a journey of courage and commitment, of resilience and renewal, and of becoming the best version of yourself. Embrace the journey with an open heart and mind, and trust in the wisdom of your intuition to guide you along the way. And remember, the true magic of the journey lies not in reaching the destination but in the transformation that occurs along the way.

Epilogue

As we come to the end of our journey through "Positive Habits: Small Steps to Big Change," we find ourselves at a crossroads—a moment of reflection and contemplation, as we look back on the path we've traveled and look forward to the road ahead. Along the way, we've explored the transformative power of positive habits, discovering how small changes in behavior can lead to profound improvements in every aspect of our lives.

Through the pages of this book, we've delved into the science of habit formation, uncovering the secrets to creating lasting change in our lives. We've learned about the importance of setting clear goals and intentions, cultivating mindfulness and self-awareness, and harnessing the power of small steps to achieve big results. We've explored practical strategies and techniques for overcoming obstacles, staying motivated, and creating a life filled with purpose, passion, and fulfillment.

But the journey doesn't end here. As we close this chapter of our lives, we are reminded that personal growth and transformation are ongoing processes—a continuous evolution of learning, growing, and becoming. The habits we've cultivated along the way are not just tools for achieving our goals; they are the building blocks of a life well-lived, the foundation upon which we can create our greatest dreams and aspirations.

As we move forward, let us carry with us the lessons we've learned and the insights we've gained. Let us continue to cultivate positive habits, nurture our growth, and strive for excellence in every area of our lives. And let us remember that change is not just something that happens to us—it's something that we have the power to create, one small step at a time.

So, as we bid farewell to this journey, let us embrace the possibilities that lie ahead with optimism, courage, and enthusiasm. Let us step boldly into the future, knowing that with the power of positive habits and the determination to pursue our dreams, anything is possible. The journey may be long, and the road may be challenging, but as long as we stay committed to our path, we can create the life of our dreams—one small step at a time.

Thank you for joining us on this journey. May your path be filled with joy, fulfillment, and endless possibilities. And may you always remember that the power to change your life lies within you.

The End.